YOUR POCKET
LIFE
COACH

☆ *May you live all the days of your life.* ☆
Jonathan Swift

D1146923

YOUR POCKET
LIFE
COACH

10 MINUTES A DAY TO TRANSFORM
YOUR LIFE AND YOUR WORK

CAROLE GASKELL

Element
An Imprint of HarperCollins*Publishers*
77–85 Fulham Palace Road
Hammersmith, London W6 8JB

The website address is: www.thorsonselement.com

and *Element* are trademarks of HarperCollins*Publishers* Ltd

Published by Thorsons, an imprint of HarperCollins*Publishers* 2001
This edition published by Element, 2003

Extracted from *Transform Your Life: 10 Steps to Real Results*
by Carole Gaskell, published by Thorsons 2000

7 9 10 8

© Carole Gaskell 2001

Carole Gaskell asserts the moral right to
be identified as the author of this work

A catalogue record for this book
is available from the British Library

ISBN 0 00 713098 8

Printed and bound in Great Britain by
Martins the Printers Ltd, Berwick upon Tweed

Contents

☆ *It only takes one person to change your life – you.* ☆

Ruth Casey

introduction

☆ *take 10 minutes a day*
to transform your life ☆

Overview

Are you optimising your potential in your life and in your work? Do you want to renew your energy, make more of your time, boost your confidence, build better relationships, shape up your finances and feel inspired to enjoy a multi-facetted, fulfilling life?

Most of us have dreams we'd like to realise, things we'd like to change, or do differently in our lives; we're full of good intentions, yet we're all so busy and the changes can seem too huge and overwhelming, that we never get around to doing anything about them. We often convince ourselves that we don't have the time, the space, the support, the resources, the money or the know-how to 'think' about what we want – let alone 'do' things differently.

Congratulations – the fact that you've bought this book means you've made the first step towards transforming your life! Each one of us can start this process in a split second, by doing something differently, taking action or thinking in a new way. You CAN transform your life, step by step, in just 10 minutes a day. You've made the perfect start, so let's get going – Your new life starts NOW!

Little and Often Leads to Success

As a lifecoach I have been a catalyst for thousands of people to transform their lives and their work, helping them to open their minds to what's possible and supporting them as they take steps to fulfil their true potential. We are all capable of making changes in our lives, the secret is to break things down into SMALL STEPS – tiny steps in fact – and spend a few minutes EVERY DAY taking action. Little and often is one of the fundamental secrets to successful transformation.

☆ *True life is lived when tiny changes occur.* ☆

Leo Tolstoy

Bite-Sized Chunks

To help make your life transformation process as effective and easy as possible, every step has been broken down into easily manageable 'bite-sized' chunks for you to tackle on a regular basis. Each quiz, question or assignment will take approximately 10 minutes of your time to complete. As you move forward 'chunk by chunk' you'll start to see things fitting together and having a significant, positive impact on your overall life. Transformation essentially involves making gradual changes and improvements from one state to another. Whether the changes you make are subtle or fundamental is up to you – even small changes can have a significant impact over the long-term! *Remember you CAN eat an elephant, but only ONE BITE AT A TIME!*

Exercise your 'Life-Changing Muscles' Regularly

This powerful pocket coach has been specifically designed for you to keep with you, follow, use and refer to on a regular basis. Like anything in life, making changes requires regular, consistent action. Think of it as exercising your 'life-changing' muscles: the more frequently you take action, the easier things become, the more steadily you progress and the quicker you start to see the results you want taking root in your life.

Make this book a part of your life over the coming weeks. Let it become a partner in your success — it is there to stimulate you, question you and challenge you. Keep it close by as you go about your daily life, write down your thoughts, your vision, your goals on the blank pages at the back, monitor your progress and let it act as a constant reminder to you that you are in charge of transforming your life.

Get into the Habit of Transformation

Ideally take one small section each day. However busy you are, you can take 10 minutes out of your hectic life each day for a good cause. If daily isn't possible for you, create a regular routine that you know will work and stick to it. Make it a habit and integrate the insights into your life moment by moment. You know you're MORE than worth it!

Quick Transformation Quiz

Answer the questions below by ticking the appropriate box and calculating your score as follows: 2 points = Yes/Agree/Not Applicable, 1 point = Agree sometimes, 0 point = No/Disagree

	YES	SOMETIMES	NO
1. My work and personal life are in balance.	❏	❏	❏
2. I have plenty of time to do the things I want.	❏	❏	❏
3. I have regular habits that support and nurture me.	❏	❏	❏
4. I am relaxed about money and/or I am earning what I deserve.	❏	❏	❏
5. I have a team of friends/family/colleagues who support me.	❏	❏	❏
6. I am self-confident and positive about life.	❏	❏	❏
7. I sleep well, eat a balanced diet and exercise as much as I need.	❏	❏	❏
8. I am excited about the future and have plans that inspire me.	❏	❏	❏
9. I have simplified my everyday life and have sufficient space for new opportunities.	❏	❏	❏
10. I am fully committed to doing what it takes to live the life I want.	❏	❏	❏

If you scored 0–10 points

You're confident with some areas of your life, but could drastically improve in others. You stand to achieve the maximum benefit from life-coaching in both your personal and your professional life. This book will help you to make the changes you want to transform your life, strengthen your support framework, establish your strengths, clarify your personal vision and tap into your true potential.

If you scored 11–15 points
Well done! Life is presumably pretty good for you. However, you probably suffer from the occasional stumbling block and suspect that you could achieve much more, both personally and professionally. This book will support you in clearing your way towards being more effective and achieving a balanced integration of your home and work life. Don't wait too long – you're almost there!

If you scored 16–20 points
Congratulations! You're obviously close to reaching your full potential. You probably know what your vision and goals are and have a plan for achieving them. This book may inspire you to achieve the last 10 or 20 per cent. This could be just the kick-start you need to go the final distance.

Ten Minutes a Day – Chapter Overview

For easy reference the book has been divided into 10 chapters:

1 Jump Start the Next Phase of Your Life

Use the past and present to help you shape your future
This first section will set you up for success by helping you to see your life in context, connecting you with your achievements, challenging you to learn from your mistakes and encouraging you to develop invaluable qualities to take your life to the next level.

2 Create a Vibrant Vision and Genuine Goals

Picture what you want, explore possibilities then be specific
Here you'll be encouraged to 'think big' as you create a vibrant vision of your future, connect with your dreams and clarify your intended outcomes, then you'll be 'focused in on specifics' as you define genuine goals and plans to move forward.

3 Build the Right Foundations

Boost your energy and surround yourself with the right people
In this chapter you'll establish a strong power base from which to launch the next phase of your life. You will be inspired to take good care of yourself, commit to regular habits and to develop a powerful support framework around you.

4 Spring Clean Your Life

De-clutter, simplify and streamline for success
As you take action in this section you'll be empowered to spring clean your life, clear the decks, and streamline your life so you gain more energy, space and clarity. You'll be encouraged to say 'No' when you need to, clean up any issues from your past and remove any distractions and obstacles likely to block your way ahead.

5 Boost Your Confidence

Know your strengths and see things in perspective
Next you will focus on your strengths and understand how others perceive you. You'll learn how to release pressure by stepping back and putting your life into perspective. You'll be inspired to do more of the things you enjoy and challenged to delegate your weaknesses so you connect more deeply with your own special essence.

6 Strengthen Your Relationships

Create ongoing positive relationships with yourself and others
Here you will focus on enhancing your life through your relationships. You'll clarify the roles and qualities of the people you want in your personal and professional life and will take action to improve your powers of communication so you can harness the power of synergy in your life.

7 Tackle Your Obstacles

Understand your blocks and take action to move forward
As you progress through this section you'll identify any potential obstacles in your way and discover what you can do to overcome them. You'll be encouraged to acknowledge the limiting beliefs that are holding you back and will be challenged to create empowering beliefs to move you forwards. If you need any tools, resources, new skills or abilities to ease your transformation you'll start taking steps to find them and to close your gaps.

8 Gain Focus and Achieve More in Less Time

Plan ahead, clarify your priorities and stay focused
A cornerstone in transforming your life is planning ahead and focusing on your priorities. The assignments in this section will enable you to hone your focus and manage yourself superbly so you achieve more in less time.

9 Shape Up Your Finances

Plug your money drains and create firm financial foundations
Next you'll be encouraged to take charge of your finances, eliminate debt and understand your emotional blocks about money. As you take action you'll be strengthening your money situation and establishing ways of propelling yourself forward financially.

10 Take Action, Maintain Momentum and Flow

Pay regular attention to your goals and celebrate your successes
Finally, you'll be pulling the whole process together, integrating your action plans into your daily life and bringing your goals into reality. You'll be inspired to step outside of your comfort zones, take advantage of synchronicity, celebrate your successes — big and small — and create real momentum to transform your life on an ongoing basis!

Enjoy the Process

There is a huge difference between understanding the theory and putting it into practice. Tackling each assignment, answering a question and identifying your action points will take you 10 minutes a day; however putting some of your insights into practice could take longer.

The real value in coaching is the role it plays in inspiring and empowering you to take ACTION to do the things you say you want to do. But once you've taken the first few steps, you (and your life) will start to gather momentum. It may take time to fully integrate all the elements of transformation but the more steps you take, the more you'll find yourself 'in the flow' and the sooner you'll start enjoying the life you really want.

☆ *The best thing about the future is that it only comes one day at a time.* ☆

Abraham Lincoln

Getting the Most out of the Exercises

You are the creator of your life – no-one else, so the more effort you put in, to answering the quizzes and questions and taking action on the assignments, the more results you're likely to achieve. Why not start now? It's never too early (or too late) to transform your life!

Familiarise Yourself with the Process

Before you start going through the steps in detail, you might find it useful to give yourself an overview by quickly skimming over the chapters to familiarise yourself with the process. The assignments themselves can be followed in sequence, or you may prefer to focus on the sections that appeal to you the most – go with whatever works best for you.

As life is constantly changing and moving in cycles, you might find you want to revisit key sections several times. The process can provide the structure for a regular review that you can re-use year after year as you perfect different elements of your life.

Make Yourself Accountable to Someone

No man is an island and one of the great benefits of lifecoaching is the synergy between the coach and client – people can often achieve a lot more by pulling their resources together and supporting each other – two heads and hearts can be greater than one. Bearing this in mind, I suggest you get the support of someone – perhaps a friend, family member, work colleague, or even a coach – as you work through this book. You'll derive great benefits from sharing your thoughts and insights with another person.

Any process of change will, at some point, bring you face to face with thoughts or issues that you would perhaps prefer not to look at. Your support person may also be able to help you with these 'growing pains'.

Your helper will act as a constant reminder to you of who you want to be and what you want to achieve. You need someone who will stand by you through thick and thin, someone you can trust to support you, hold you to your commitments and keep you on track.

I will make myself accountable to: _____

Allow Yourself 'Quiet Time' to Think Things Through

As you work through a specific assignment you might want to stop and ponder for a while. I actively encourage you to do this. Sometimes, it's during the gaps between our thoughts that we gain the real insights and answers to our life's questions.

To do this, I suggest that you take yourself to a quiet inspirational place in your home. Play your favourite music, sit in your favourite chair, light a candle, look at your favourite view – do whatever is necessary to fully access your thoughts. If you prefer, a visit to your local café or park or a drive in your car might spark your imagination and give you the answers you're looking for. Remember the answers are inside you, so the more comfortable and 'at one' you feel with your environment, the easier you'll find it to open yourself up, increase your awareness and draw the answers to you.

Keep Your Insights in a Journal or Notebook

As you work through *Your Pocket Life Coach* you'll probably want to make notes or jot down the answers to the questions. You can use the blank pages at the back of this book or a journal or notebook – why not treat yourself to one now, before you begin?

Confirm Your Commitment

As you begin the lifecoaching process, it's important to acknowledge that whilst ideas, dreams and goals have a valuable place in your life, they're only as good as your commitment to achieving them. Are you ready to start taking the steps required to turn your ideas into reality?

☆ How committed are you to transforming your life? Rate yourself on a scale of 1 to 10. 1 being not committed at all and 10 being totally committed.
   1 2 3 4 5 6 7 8 9 10

☆ How committed are you to actively participating in the exercises in this book? Again 1 is not committed and 10 totally committed.
   1 2 3 4 5 6 7 8 9 10

☆ What will you do to keep yourself disciplined to follow this process?

Now you're ready to get going, read and sign the following agreement. Here's to transforming your life! Enjoy it!
Carole Gaskell

☆ *Man's mind stretched to a new idea never goes back to its original shape.* ☆

Oliver Wendell Holmes

My Agreement to Transform my Life

I .... am committed to transforming my life. I understand I will get out of the process as much I put into it and that it's up to me to create my own value from each of the assignments.

I acknowledge that a lot will be asked of me. I am willing to experiment with changing my behaviour; trying new things; reassessing the assumptions and perceptions I hold; setting goals that are bigger; removing sources of stress in my life and starting to redesign the way I spend my time. I agree to complete the assignments to the best of my ability and to take action on the plans I write.

I commit to devoting .... hours/days/weeks to transform my life.

I will be honest with myself when the going gets tough and will ask for support when I realise I need it. Above all else I will relax, take time and enjoy the process.

....
Your signature here   Date

☆ *Until one is committed there is hesitancy, the chance to draw back, always ineffectiveness. Concerning all acts of initiative (and creation) there is one elementary truth, the ignorance of which kills countless ideas and splendid plans: the moment one definitely commits oneself, then Providence moves too. All sorts of things occur to help one that would otherwise never have occurred. A whole stream of events issues from the decision, raising in one's favour all manner of unforeseen incidents and meetings and material assistance, which no man could have dreamed would have come his way.* ☆

W. N. Murray, The Scottish Himalayan Expedition.

☆ *And the day came when the risk it took to remain tight in a bud was more painful than the risk it took to blossom.* ☆

Anaïs Nin

☆ 1 jump start
the next phase
of your life

☆ *use the past and present*
to help you shape your future ☆

Overview

If you're ready to embark on the next chapter of your life, you've come to the right place. You probably feel a combination of excitement, fear, hope, expectation – and a host of other emotions, this is perfectly normal. I simply ask that you approach the lifecoaching process with an open mind, be willing to 'have a go' at the exercises and become aware of the thoughts, feelings and insights that come up for you.

The chances are, by this current stage in your life, you've already gained some incredibly valuable life experiences – some positive and others negative – but however you look at them, they all provide useful pointers for your future. I want you to reflect on these experiences and use them to your advantage to jump start the next phase of your life.

As you work through the 10-minute assignments in this section, you'll be setting yourself up to tackle the remaining steps more easily.

This first section will set you up for success by:

☆ helping you to see your life in context
☆ reminding you of your achievements
☆ challenging you to learn from your disappointments
☆ empowering you to learn from your mistakes
☆ triggering you to notice areas for improvement
☆ encouraging you to develop invaluable qualities within yourself, to take your life to the next level.

Quick Transformation Quiz

Answer the questions below by ticking the appropriate box and calculating your score as follows: 2 points = Yes/Agree/Not Applicable, 1 point = Agree sometimes, 0 point = No/Disagree

	YES	SOMETIMES	NO
1. I take full responsibility for what happens to me in life.	❑	❑	☑
2. I know I always have a choice.	❑	❑	☑
3. I have a positive attitude to life.	❑	❑	☑
4. I can always be counted on to follow through and to meet previously agreed expectations.	❑	❑	☑
5. I am honest and truthful with myself.	❑	☑	❑
6. I am courageous and have plenty of inner strength.	☑	❑	❑
7. I hold myself accountable and keep my word 99 per cent of the time.	❑	❑	☑
8. I am able to sit back when necessary and see the bigger picture of my life.	❑	❑	☑
9. I am fully aware of my key accomplishments in life.	❑	❑	☑
10. I am willing to learn lessons from my life's disappointments.	☑	❑	❑

☆ *Insanity is doing the same thing over and over again and expecting different results.* ☆

Albert Einstein

Achievements

If you cast your mind back over the past few years, what were your three biggest achievements? We are often so busy looking forward, to what's next in our lives, that we forget to acknowledge our very real progress to date. Here I want you to fully recognise your accomplishments, embrace them, strengthen yourself and allow yourself to expand as a result.

☆ Achievement 1 KIT

☆ Achievement 2 GETTING ON HNC

☆ Achievement 3 GETTING/STAYING SOBER.

Identifying your most significant moments is a valuable first step, acknowledging them as such is the next. Giving yourself a pat on the back is important, as it connects you with your strengths and helps you to focus on the positive elements of your life, enhancing your personal energy and spark. As you go through a process of change, I want you to notice the milestones along the way. I want you to notice and enjoy the journey of life step by step. The more you do this on an ongoing basis, the easier you'll find it to build momentum for the things you want to do and create in your life.

Your Challenges and Disappointments

An essential part of valuing yourself and understanding your true essence is to connect with what you already know about yourself. Our challenges, mistakes and disappointments also highlight a lot about how we work and understand ourselves. I would like you to spend the next 10 minutes writing down your answers to the following questions:

☆ What have been your greatest concerns or challenges in recent years and how have you overcome them?

☆ What have been your biggest disappointments in recent years and why?

 Your Top Three Lessons

Casting your mind back over your experiences, what have you learnt from them? Why do you think these events occurred? What were they trying to teach you? If you had your time again, is there anything you would have done differently? Each of us is the expert on our own life and if we allow ourselves the time to reflect, we can access our own wisdom to move us forward. Give yourself 10 minutes to come up with the three most valuable pieces of advice you could give yourself, to enable you to get the most out of this new phase of life.

☆ The three most valuable pieces of advice that would make the biggest difference to me in the year ahead are:

☆ What are the three lessons you've learned from your accomplishments and/or disappointments that you think would have the greatest impact on you if you implemented them into the next phase of your life?

☆ *Learn to get in touch with the silence within yourself, and know that everything in this life has purpose. There are no mistakes, no coincidences. All events are blessings given to us to learn from.* ☆

Elizabeth Kubler-Ross

Quick Tip

Adopt a Positive Attitude

Adopt a positive outlook on life and a 'can do' attitude. Remember you are responsible for your own thoughts, it's your choice whether the cup is half-full or half-empty. Choose to have a good day and choose to be proactive. Positivity is catching, so spread it to those around you and see yourself naturally propelled onwards and upwards.

Act Deliberately

Rather than spend your time reacting to external demands from other people or letting situations dictate your actions, instead choose to act deliberately from your own centre of calm. When you act deliberately you come from a knowing deep within you, where you are centred and in-tune with yourself and your own needs. You can do this by closely monitoring your every action, becoming mindful of your thoughts and reactions on a moment by moment basis and acting in accordance with the wisdom inside you. Try this for the next week and you'll be amazed how much more effective you become and how much you strengthen your confidence in yourself.

4 This Year's Progress

Look back over the last year. You will have had some great accomplishments, maybe a few disappointments and no doubt the odd challenge. Where have they brought you? If you look at your life at the moment, is there anything that you can do now that last year you wouldn't have dreamed of being able to do?

☆ Write a list of three things from both your personal and professional life which illustrate the progress you have made in the last year. This could be anything from learning to drive to giving a nerve-free presentation.

 5 Influential People

The people around us can have a profound effect on the way we look at our lives, especially those who influence and inspire us, personally or professionally. Take 10 minutes now to think about which people have been the most influential in your a) personal life and b) professional life over the past year? What is it about them that has impacted on your life? Do they have characteristics that you wish you had yourself?

⑥ Role Models

We often have role models or heroes – sometimes it is their image we aspire to, the way they deal with other people, how they communicate or their work that inspires us.

☆ Learning from role models can be a great way of developing yourself. Be aware of people who impress you for a particular reason, ask yourself why and what you can learn from this particular person. Can you modify what they do to suit your own personality? You may find it useful to read autobiographies of successful people, listen to tapes, go to workshops – do whatever will support and inspire you.

☆ Who are your top three heroes or role models (alive or dead)? What do you admire most about them and why?

☆ I admire them because:

☆ The qualities I would like to emulate are:

☆ I will do this by:

7 The Wheel of Life

The eight sections of the Wheel of Life represent a balanced wheel. Take the centre or hub of the wheel as 0 (totally dissatisfied) and the outer edge as 10 (totally satisfied). Rank your level of satisfaction with each area of your life by putting a cross on the relevant spoke. Draw a line to join the crosses together.

How balanced does the shape of your wheel look? Which of the areas of your life are you currently happy with? Where do you want to make improvements? (You might want to refer back to this wheel when you answer the questions in Chapter Two.)

Wheel of Life

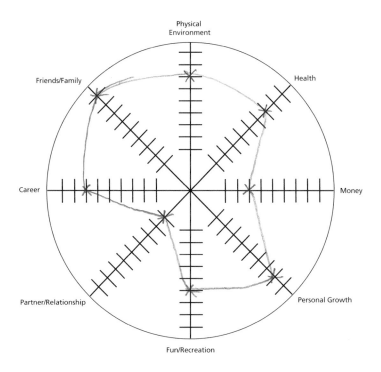

⭐ 8 Wheel of Success

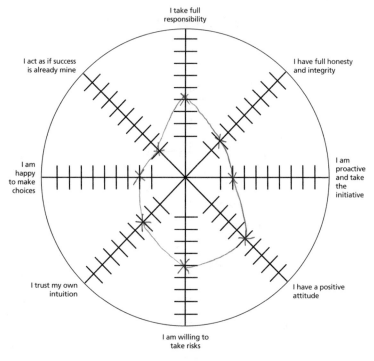

The Wheel of Success encourages you to develop invaluable qualities within yourself to take your life to the next level.

☆ The eight sections represent key characteristics of success. Take the centre, or hub, of the wheel as 0 (not true for me now) and the outer edges as 10 (totally true for me now). Rate yourself currently, by putting a cross on the relevant spoke. Draw a line to join the crosses. How balanced does the perimeter of your wheel look? Which of the characteristics would you like to work on? What will you do to embrace these qualities during this new phase of your life?

Remember, taking time to savour your past and clarify your present will revitalise you for the next phase ahead. Reflecting on the events and people who have shaped you, and understanding and being honest with yourself about your current reality, will enable you to see where you want to go and help you set yourself up for a fabulous year ahead. Well done for completing Chapter One!

9 Putting Your Life into Perspective

While you're in the preparation stage of jump starting the next phase of your life, you'll find this next 10-minute exercise incredibly useful in helping you to see your life from a fresh vantage point. Sit down quietly and fast-forward your life. Imagine it's your eightieth birthday. You are celebrating with family and friends. Take time to review your life as the 80-year-old you. What have you achieved in your life? What do you feel proud of? What is it about you that people value? What are the most significant elements that you are celebrating?

☆ *Change your thoughts and you change your world.* ☆

Norman Vincent Peale

2 create a
vibrant vision
and genuine goals

☆ *picture what you want, explore*
possibilities then be specific ☆

Overview

The fun starts here! Your vision is the overriding picture of the life you're aiming towards. It's an inspiring way of looking to your future. Having a vision brings you the opportunity to focus on what's truly important to you.

☆ *Your vision will become clear only when you can look into your own heart. Who looks outside, dreams; who looks inside, awakens.* ☆

Carl Jung

The more 'vibrant' you make your vision, the more easily you'll find it coming to life. It really is up to you what you paint on the tapestry of your life and how you want your transformation to look. Your intentions, dreams and desires are the very essence of you.

The time you spend working on the assignments in this section will be invaluable in helping you to shape your destiny.

When you've completed this chapter:

☆ You'll have developed a vibrant vision of your future
☆ You'll have set genuine goals, for your personal and professional life
☆ You'll have made your goals SMART and will understand the benefits, pain and strengths associated with each goal
☆ You'll have started to break your goals down into small steps
☆ You'll be paying attention to and taking daily action towards moving your goals forward.

Quick Transformation Quiz

Answer the questions below by ticking the appropriate box and calculating your score as follows: 2 points = Yes/Agree/Not Applicable, 1 point = Agree sometimes, 0 point = No/Disagree

	YES	SOMETIMES	NO
1. I have a clear vision of the life and work I want to create.	❑	❑	❑
2. I can picture the results I want to achieve in my life.	❑	❑	❑
3. I am willing and able to stretch myself and to commit to something bigger than myself.	❑	❑	❑
4. I acknowledge that life moves in cycles and I have a clear theme for the current cycle I am in.	❑	❑	❑
5. I spend valuable time in silence/inner reflection and/or meditation to think about my life.	❑	❑	❑
6. I am clear about my personal and professional goals.	❑	❑	❑
7. I am clear about the reasons why I want to achieve my goals.	❑	❑	❑
8. I am aware of the thoughts, beliefs or other obstacles that are blocking me from achieving my goals and am taking action to deal with them.	❑	❑	❑
9. I have established specific action plans and timescales for each goal.	❑	❑	❑
10. I revisit my goals on a regular basis and am taking progressive steps towards them.	❑	❑	❑

Develop a Vibrant Vision of Your Future

It can be difficult to see with any great certainty into the future. You may not know what your life is going to look like one year from now, let alone in three or five years' time. However, the more you think about the way you want your life to be, the more chance you have of developing a plan that is going to bring you happiness. Many business people are familiar with the concept of vision from a work perspective, but surprisingly few of us actually apply it to our own life. I want you to be clear about your vision before you go any further.

Put Things into Perspective

Having a powerful vision helps you to put the rest of your life into perspective and will make the day-to-day pressures and small setbacks seem less important.

When your vision is really compelling, you even find yourself being pulled effortlessly towards it, rather than striving to make things happen. You can let your own vision gently pull you forward to the future of your dreams!

Develop your Three-Year Vision

I would like you to start by focusing specifically on the next three years. Imagine you're revisiting this book three years from now. Allow yourself to look back over the last three years of your life to the present day.

☆ What would have to have happened over the past three years, both in my personal and work life, for me to feel happy and pleased with my progress?

☆ Give yourself 10 minutes or so to jot down your thoughts about how you want your life to be. Write everything down in the present tense and be as specific as you can.

☆ How do you feel? Who are you as a person? Describe as best as you can what will have to happen for you to be happy in the knowledge that you've achieved your desired results.

My Vision for my Life

☆ Describe the following in as much detail as you can:
Personal life, home and family
Work/business life
Health and well-being
Finances
Relationships and community
Intellectual and/or spiritual life
Any other important elements

Quick Tip

'White Space'

An incredibly useful habit many of my clients derive great benefit from is creating 15 minutes of 'white space' each day. What I mean by 'white space' is totally silent time when you simply do nothing, just quieten your mind and be still for 15 minutes. You might like to sit quietly or meditate. Whatever you do, just allowing yourself some quiet time gives you the opportunity to get in touch with your inner self. If you find the prospect of 15 minutes a little daunting, start with five minutes and gradually build up. Or do more if it works for you! You may be surprised how refreshed and inspired you feel afterwards.

Some people find doing this first thing in the morning is the perfect way of setting up the day, while for others it may be after lunch or last thing at night.

 Create a Destiny Map

You may find that a useful way of clarifying your vision is to create a destiny map, a visual representation of what you would like in your life. It can help you to make your dreams tangible by using pictures and symbols to create reality. A useful timeframe to use in a destiny map is between one and three years.

To create your own destiny map, get yourself a large poster board. You'll need a wide variety of magazines, pictures, crayons, glue, scissors and anything else you think might be useful in starting to create pictorially the life you want to live.

Simply go through the magazines and cut out any images or symbols that represent the things you would like in your life – a house in the country, a specific type of car, a family you would like to have, pictures of the sort of work you would like to be doing or hobbies you would like to pursue. Stick the pictures on the board and create a collage of your new life.

How much money would you like to be earning? Some people find that pinning either Monopoly money or bank notes on the board or even writing themselves out a cheque for the amount of money they would like to be earning focuses their mind on what it is they'd like to create. Build your picture as fully and as colourfully as you can. Don't make the board too cluttered, keep it clear and focused on the key elements – unless you want your life to be cluttered!

This can be a really fun exercise to do and the more focused your attention and the more energy you put into it, the more powerful your destiny map will be. You may find you want to have a go with friends, and let them create their maps while you're creating yours. Some people like to create a destiny map as part of their meditation process, when they sit quietly and let the thoughts come to them and then find the images and the pictures to create their own boards.

Once you've completed the destiny map, put it in a place where you can look at it regularly. Let it become a constant reminder of how you want your life to be. A good idea is to look at it just before you go to bed and then allow your sub-conscious mind to work on it while you sleep.

3 Know your Outcome at the Beginning

One of the key principles of success is to know your outcome, what you want to achieve. It's only by understanding your objectives that you can work out the relevant strategy to achieve them. Also, knowing your desired outcome helps to keep you on track when you start to focus on the details. Spend 10 minutes answering the following questions:

☆ How, specifically, will you know that your time spent following the transformation process will have been worthwhile? What would have *happened* in your life?

☆ If there was one important *change* that you could make in the next three months, what would it be?

 4 Create a Theme

If you could give this next phase of your life transformation an overall theme, what would it be? (Examples could include 'Creating Space for Me', 'Developing a Life I Love', 'Moving my Business to the Next Level', 'Attracting my Ideal Life Partner' and so on.) Creating a theme will help you visualize and work towards your goals.

☆ My theme is:

Three Personal Goals

When you set the right goals for yourself, you will feel excited, a little nervous, ready and willing to go for it.

☆ List three *specific* goals you want to achieve over the next year.

☆ List three *specific* goals you want to achieve in the next three months.

 Three Professional Goals

Now turn your attention towards the workplace. List three specific goals you want to achieve in your professional life over the next year. Then focus more on the short term and consider what specific goals are attainable in the next three months.

☆ List three *specific* professional goals you want to achieve over the next year.

☆ List three *specific* professional goals you want to achieve over the next three months.

7 Make your Goals SMART and Genuine

SMART means making your goals Specific, Measurable, Attainable and Realistic within a given Timeframe.

Be specific and detailed about what you want and where possible quantify each goal, so you can easily measure your progress. Be realistic and set goals that are within reach (even if that requires effort on your part). If you set your goals too high, you may become discouraged; conversely, if you set them too low, they won't stretch you enough. I don't want you to lose motivation or the momentum needed to make them happen.

Ensure your Goals Are Genuine

The following is a quick checklist to ensure you've clarified the right goals. Ask yourself the questions below to check that your goals are in alignment with who you are and what you really want:

☆ *Does this goal keep me moving towards who I want to be?*
Ensure that your goals are in harmony with the overall theme of your life and don't detract from it.

☆ *Are my goals in alignment with my values?*
Make sure you're not working towards a goal that conflicts with your values. If your goals are consistent with your own inner beliefs, your ability to achieve them will never be undermined.

☆ *Do my goals truly come from my heart and not just my head?*
Ensure that each goal is something you genuinely want rather than
something someone else thinks you should have. If the goal is right
for you you'll find synchronicity starts to step in. (We'll talk about this
more in Chapter 10.)

8 Benefits, Pains and Strengths

You can't underestimate the power of intention. It's your intention to do
something that will really bring about conscious change. The energy from
your intention itself has the power to organize events and make it happen.
As Deepak Chopra says in his *Seven Spiritual Laws of Success* 'Through your
intent, you can literally command the Laws of Nature to fulfil your dreams
and desires.'

For each goal, ask yourself, 'If I attain this, what will it give me?' Take
some time to write down the *big benefit* of achieving each goal. If ever you
falter when working towards a goal, reminding yourself of the big benefit
will help to keep you motivated.

☆ What is the big benefit of accomplishing each goal?

When you've written your list, put it in your diary or journal or post it on
the fridge or the mirror in your bathroom, wherever you're going to look at
it regularly.

☆ *Destiny is not a matter of chance, it is a matter of choice. It is not a thing to be waited for, it is a thing to be achieved.* ☆

Jeremy Kitson

Identify the Pain of Not Achieving Each Goal

Connecting strongly with the benefits of achieving a certain goal is a powerful way to keep yourself motivated. However sometimes reminding yourself of the pain you're likely to feel by *not* accomplishing the goal could be an even stronger incentive. Remember, the more you get in touch with what it's costing you to stay where you are, the easier you'll find it to overcome any obstacles in your way.

☆ Look back at your goals list and write down the pain associated in not accomplishing each of your goals.

☆ *The thoughts we choose to think are the tools we use to paint the canvas of our lives.* ☆

Louise Hay

9 Break your Goals into Steps

The goals you've selected may be large or small. The chances are, if you're serious about transforming your life, some of your goals are likely to be big ones. Good for you – congratulations on setting yourself a challenge!

I don't want you feel overwhelmed by any of your goals. Breaking your goals down into manageable chunks helps you to devise sensible action plans for them. Setting intermediate targets helps you make a start and build momentum. If you want to achieve a certain weight loss in a specific period of time, for example, you might want to break that goal down into weekly and monthly goals.

The motivational expert Napoleon Hill said, 'Conceive, believe, achieve.' If you believe you can achieve something, you will. Simply take your first steps towards it and as you become more confident, the subsequent steps become easier.

Develop a Three-Step Action Plan for each Goal

☆ List below the first three action steps you're willing and ready to take to move each of your key goals forward:

Personal Goal 1   Professional Goal 1
☆   ☆
☆   ☆
☆   ☆

Personal Goal 2	Professional Goal 2
☆	☆
☆	☆
☆	☆

Personal Goal 3	Professional Goal 3
☆	☆
☆	☆
☆	☆

☆ *The greatest danger for most of us is not that our aim is too high and we miss it, but that it is too low and we reach it.* ☆

Unknown

☆3 build
the right
foundations

☆ *boost your energy and surround*
yourself with the right people ☆

Overview

If you want to transform your life and turn your dreams into reality, it goes without saying that you need to develop the right foundations first. A skyscraper requires firm foundations from which it can tower into the sky. I want you to create the strongest foundations possible on which to build your life.

As you work through the assignments in this chapter I want you to make sure you're taking the best possible care of yourself. You'll be encouraged to integrate regular habits into your life and to build a strong framework of people and resources to support you.

You may be tempted to charge ahead with goals and plans, but the time you spend on creating your foundations is an investment that will pay off for the rest of your life.

When you've completed this chapter:

☆ You'll be taking exceptional care of your physical, mental and emotional wellbeing

☆ You'll have established regular habits to support you for the rest of your life

☆ You'll be boosting your energy regularly by doing more of the things you enjoy

☆ You'll have identified a team of spark people to inspire you

☆ You'll have actively engaged the support of key people to help you as you transform your life

☆ You'll have set up invaluable systems and resources to make your life easier.

Quick Transformation Quiz

*Answer the questions below by ticking the appropriate box and calculating your score as
follows: 2 points = Yes/Agree/Not Applicable, 1 point = Agree sometimes, 0 point =
No/Disagree*

	YES	SOMETIMES	NO
1. My body is in good shape, I'm happy with my weight and I exercise regularly, so I have lots of energy and vitality.	☐	☑	☐
2. I eat plenty of healthy food for sustenance and pleasure but not for emotional comfort. I am not abusing my body with too much alcohol, caffeine or drugs.	☐	☑	☐
3. I have created a tranquil, harmonious home, filled with the furniture, decor, art and music I love.	☐	☐	☑
4. I only wear clothes that make me feel good and I have a haircut that makes me feel great.	☐	☑	☐
5. I have had a physical examination within the last three years and my cholesterol and blood pressure are at a healthy level.	☑	☐	☐
6. I visit my dentist and optician regularly to ensure my eyes and teeth are healthy.	☐	☐	☑
7. I have as much sleep as I need to function happily.	☐	☑	☐
8. I have things to look forward to and smile and laugh out loud every day.	☐	☑	☐
9. I have regular breaks, take evenings and weekends off and use my holiday entitlement for pure relaxation (no chores).	☐	☑	☐
10. I receive plenty of love from people around me and tell them how they can support and help me.	☑	☐	☐

Self-care and Self-full

If you want to transform your life, you need to transform yourself first. To do this, it's important to make self-care your number one priority.

I'd like to make a distinction here between self-care and being selfish, as these two terms are quite different. Some people feel uncomfortable about putting their own self-care first, thinking it a very selfish way of behaving. From a coaching point of view, self-care is a 'self-full' activity, not a 'self-ish' one. The more you work on yourself, invest in yourself, take care of yourself and fill your own cup, the more you have to give others. I actually believe it's selfish *not* to take care of yourself first. When you neglect yourself you're running on empty tanks, which drains energy from other people rather than supports them. Remember, you can't give what you don't have, so unless you love and nurture yourself first, you won't be able to give these gifts to others.

How did you score your health and wellbeing on the Wheel of Life in Chapter One?

How did you score on the Transformation Quiz? You've probably already gained a few clues about how you can take better care of yourself.

☆ List the ways you're currently taking care of yourself. What are you doing to put yourself first?

Surprisingly few of us are as kind to ourselves as we'd like to be. Late nights, excessive eating, drinking, smoking and other bad habits don't do you any favours. I challenge you to *act* now to take the best possible care of yourself – for a start, why not book yourself in for a massage, spend more time with friends, have a fabulous haircut or do more of something you really enjoy?

☆ *Invent your world. Surround yourself with people, colour, sounds and work that nourish you.* ☆

Sark

2 Identify 10 Joys in your Life

These are an important part of your self-care and a fabulous way of nurturing your soul. I want you to ensure you are sprinkling plenty of music, humour, dance, interests and hobbies over your life so you have something to look forward to every day. It goes without saying that the more you fill your life with things you enjoy – big or small – the greater your sense of contentment will be.

What are the things that give you a real sense of joy? Perhaps for you it's spending quality time with your children or sleeping on freshly laundered bedding, playing tennis or having fresh flowers and candles in your home.

☆ What changes do you want to make to sprinkle more fun and inspiration over your life?

☆ List your top 10 joys.

⭐3 Chain Reaction

Being proactive means taking the initiative and not waiting for things to happen to you. People who are successful in life tend to be proactive – they are aware every day that the life they live is their own choice. It's not so much what happens to you in life that's important – it's what you do with what happens. Equally, it's not so much how you fall down that matters, but how you get up again!

☆ What could you stop – or start doing that would trigger a beneficial chain of events?

⭐4 Ten Regular Habits

One of the best ways to start integrating life-enhancing activities into your day-to-day life is to establish regular habits – things you agree to do daily, weekly or monthly for the foreseeable future.

These habits can be small, but if carried out on a regular basis will greatly enhance your life. Possible suggestions include exercising for at least 20 minutes every day (whether that's a brisk walk or a workout in the gym is entirely up to you!), having at least seven to eight hours sleep every night, drinking a couple of litres of water a day, having a real laugh with someone each day, having a fortnightly massage, making three new work contacts each week, returning phone calls immediately, reading an inspirational poem or smiling at a stranger at least once a day.

☆ Think about the 10 regular habits you want to take up that will support you in being the person you want to be, living the life you really want.

5 Imagine a Life with No Obstacles

☆ If you were totally financially independent and money wasn't an issue for you, what would your life be like? How would you spend your time? Likewise, if you knew you couldn't fail, what would you be doing differently in your life? Take 10 minutes now to write down your answers, remove yourself from the constraints of your day-to-day life and think 'large'. Then read back over your responses and see what you have learnt about yourself.

6 Daily Inspiration Journal

As one of your regular habits, I actively encourage you to maintain a daily inspiration journal. Keeping a diary or journal to record your thoughts, insights, intuitive ideas and actions as your new life unfolds will support you profoundly during your transformation process. Not only will it help you to clarify your thoughts and build your confidence in yourself, but it will also serve as a very interesting memento to refer back to from time to time, so you really can see how far you've progressed!

Updating your daily inspiration journal will require self-discipline at first, but please persist. Once you get into the routine of making your daily entries, you'll find the five or 10 minutes it takes will greatly enhance your life. Treat yourself to a notebook or diary that inspires you and start writing today!

Some people find it beneficial to make entries in their journal briefly twice a day, in the morning and at night. You might prefer to choose just one of these times.

You might include your thoughts on the following:

☆ things about the day that make you feel happy/confident/excited
☆ things that you appreciate, are proud of or are committed to doing
☆ people and things in the day that you love and why
☆ things that may not be quite right but which you have plans to change
☆ things you have learned in the day or that have helped you to develop in some way.

If you want to keep your inspiration journal really focused, why not write down your top three 'big wins' – the three key things that have been the highlights of your day?

Once you become disciplined about keeping your journal you'll find yourself gaining a heightened sense of awareness of what makes you happy and will become more appreciative of some of the simple things in your life. The real benefits come when you start to take action on your discoveries by doing more of the things you enjoy and less of those you don't! Try to keep a daily inspiration journal for the next month and see how it enhances your life! Remember, gratitude is the attitude which determines your altitude!

 **Spark People**

Spark people are those who do just that – they spark you off with new ideas, they inspire you, challenge you, stretch you and encourage you to be all you can be and more. These people play an essential role in your own growth.

☆ Who has been a spark person for you in your life? Why and how did they achieve that?

☆ Who do you want to invite onto your spark team for the next phase of your life?

The more you surround yourself with successful, inspirational people, the more you'll learn and the greater the likelihood that some of it may rub off on you!

☆ *Often people attempt to live their lives backwards; they try to have more things, or more money, in order to do more of what they want so they will be happier. The way it actually works is the reverse. You must first BE who you really are, then, DO what you need to do, in order to HAVE what you want.* ☆

Margaret Young

Quick Tip

Develop a Strong Sense of Personal Integrity & Honesty

Life becomes significantly easier when you're able to live honestly with yourself. When you fully master this quality, few things can really threaten you. You'll find you have fewer problems and possess an innate sense of inner peace and calm. When you know and accept yourself for who you are as a person and are genuinely giving of your best, you don't have to waste your time and energy trying to be anything else.

Being 'in integrity' means not only accepting responsibility for your actions, but also being true to yourself, having self-respect and taking good care of all aspects of your physical, mental, emotional and spiritual being. Are you doing the best for yourself and your body? Are you stressed out? Are you eating and/or drinking too much? Are you running on adrenaline? Are you overlooking problems? Are you avoiding telling the truth? Are you not taking adequate time for yourself?

A person who is 'out of integrity' is like someone whose spine is out of alignment – their total being is unable to operate at its optimum capability. When your life is out of integrity, things tend to go wrong and you're highly likely to blame others. You'll know when you're out of integrity because there are significant gaps between what you say and what you do.

You can start to enhance your own personal integrity by identifying 10 areas of your life where you're not currently telling the full truth – either to yourself or others. List them and then write next to each one the actions you will take to address it and the date by which you will have completed them.

I'd like you to tackle two of these issues each week over the next month or so until you know you're living a fully authentic life.

 ## Fundamental Support People

Fundamental support people are those you connect with in your inner circle of friends, family and associates who you know you can totally rely on to be there to support you as you move your life forwards.

☆ Who has been a fundamental support for you in your life? Why and how did they achieve this? What specifically is it about them that you valued?

☆ Who do you want to invite onto your fundamental support team to help move you forward with the next phase of your life?

☆ If you could learn from anyone, who would it be? Why?

Once you've identified your inner team, tell each person individually how they can help you most and really acknowledge for them the role they are about to play in your life.

9 Identify Resources to Support You

The final element in developing your foundations is ensuring you have the right physical resources around you to operate at your best. What do you need to enhance your life – tools, machinery, electrical equipment, lighting, a computer, dishwasher, fridge-freezer, furniture, car, stereo? Take 10 minutes to answer the following questions and put a date by which you will commit to action.

☆ What resources would enhance your home life?

☆ What resources would enhance your work life?

☆ What systems do you need to help you operate at your best?

☆ What resources can you surround yourself with to optimize your performance, productivity and sense of fulfilment?

☆ What else would be useful to you (information, books, life-skills, knowledge, etc)?

4 spring
clean
your life

☆ *de-clutter, simplify and*
streamline for success ☆

Overview

If you want to make fundamental changes in your life you need to have enough space and time to do so. This next step is crucial in clearing your path ahead. As a coach, I often spend my early sessions with clients helping them to create more space, time and clarity in their lives, before we embark on achieving their more ambitious goals. Clarity often only comes after we've given our lives a bit of a 'spring clean'.

Once you've cleared the decks, removed any unnecessary clutter, noise, distractions and energy-drainers from your life and have started to say 'No' to everything except your most important priorities, only then will you have sufficient space for the good and positive things to come into your life.

As you tackle the assignments in this section you'll be creating more physical, mental and emotional space for the next phase of your life. Your future will move in faster once you've cleared space for it!

When you've completed this chapter:

☆ You'll have de-cluttered your home and work environment
☆ You'll have addressed many of the small, niggly, energy-drainers you've been putting up with in your life
☆ You'll be saying 'No' more often
☆ You'll have simplified, organized and streamlined your life
☆ You'll have cleaned up issues from your past, so you can be more present in the moment and able to pay attention and enjoy the 'now'
☆ You'll be building reserves, so you have more than enough time, space and energy for new possibilities.

Quick Transformation Quiz

Answer the questions below by ticking the appropriate box and calculating your score as follows: 2 points = Yes/Agree/Not Applicable, 1 point = Agree sometimes, 0 point = No/Disagree

	YES	SOMETIMES	NO
1. My home and work environments are de-cluttered and inspiring.	❏	❏	❏
2. My wardrobe and drawers are well-organized and my clothes are cleaned and ironed.	❏	❏	❏
3. My paperwork, correspondence and receipts are filed away neatly.	❏	❏	❏
4. I am not putting up with anything in my home or work environment that niggles or annoys me.	❏	❏	❏
5. I don't have a lot of things hanging in the air, unfinished projects, business matters or other items.	❏	❏	❏
6. I never do something because I feel I should or ought to.	❏	❏	❏
7. I don't overload my life with too much television and radio or too many newspapers.	❏	❏	❏
8. I have let go of people and relationships that drag me down or have a negative influence over me.	❏	❏	❏
9. I have cleaned up issues from my past and am able to be more 'present' in the now.	❏	❏	❏
10. I am building reserves for myself so that I have more time and energy for new possibilities.	❏	❏	❏

1 De-clutter and Create an Inspirational Environment at Home and at Work

Developing an inspirational environment, both at home and at work, is a key element of your launch pad. I want you to create a tranquil, harmonious home as one of the cornerstones of your life. If the space you inhabit has a positive atmosphere, you're more likely to be in a position to operate at your best.

Do you like the area where you live? Do you like the area where you work? If it's not ideal, what can you do to make the best of it? Is your home somewhere you can relax and recharge? Does it suit your preferred lifestyle? Are you happy with the layout, the furniture, the decor?

Sometimes small changes at home – painting a wall, putting a candle in the bedroom, changing the lighting, adding shelving, fresh flowers, music, pictures – can make a big difference. At work, adding plants and making sure you have a clear desk and tidy files can give you more energy to be productive. Think what you can do to improve your own space.

☆ What changes do you want to make to your home?

☆ What changes do you want to make to the area where you work?

De-sludge your Life

We all have a certain amount of 'sludge' in our lives – issues, people and beliefs that block us, slow us down or drain our energy. We put up with clutter, niggly unfinished tasks and 'less than ideal' situations that divert us from the important things in life. If you want to be clear about your future, you need to get rid of as much of this 'sludge' as possible.

What are the niggles, big and small, in your life at this moment? Maybe you haven't really noticed until now all the little annoying things that are holding you back. We tolerate so many things unnecessarily. A negative friend, a faulty vacuum cleaner, a freezer that's too small, a photocopier that doesn't work properly, a pile of ironing, unfinished paperwork, a wilting plant, a dirty car, a client who wears us down – the list is endless!

☆ Make a list of the top 10 things that you're putting up with.

☆ Select two of these, address them and eliminate them by the end of this week.

Revisit your list and put a date by the side of each issue to confirm when you will have resolved it. Gradually, one by one, work at eliminating them. You'll find this process is ongoing. As you address certain niggles, new ones may crop up. An effective way of managing this is to develop a system for keeping on top of things. Perhaps you can set aside a specific time each week to tackle niggles and agree areas of responsibility with the people around you at home and/or work.

As you start to get rid of things you've been putting up with, you'll feel lighter and have more energy. The more actions you take, the more positive the space around you will become and the clearer your path ahead will appear!

 3 **Remove the Energy Drainers**

A major benefit in spring cleaning your life is the boost it provides to your energy flow. Successful people have more than enough energy – mental, physical and emotional – to carry their ideas and projects through to completion. Their energy visibly flows through them and can be contagious, captivating others and sweeping them along as things get done in double-quick time. To optimize your energy flow, you need to minimize your energy drains and maximize the energy coming into your life.

Clutter drains you of energy, so sort everything out, decide what to keep, throw out, give away, sell or store. Get rid of anything you don't absolutely need or haven't used in the last 12 months. Assign a home to everything you wish to keep and get organized to prevent the build up from occurring again. De-junk your entire life – cut down on TV, newspapers and information overload. Cancel subscriptions to publications you don't have the time to read. Limit your Internet access. Cut down on alcohol and junk food. Detox your body and your mind and blitz your environment. Keep asking yourself, 'What else can I do to simplify my life?'

☆ Is there anything draining your energy at this moment? If anything has escaped from your previous list, write it down now, together with a plan for eliminating it:

4 Say 'No' More Often

'No' is an extremely powerful word which, in the early stages of transforming your life, can be most useful. The lifecoaching process itself encourages you to be positive and proactive. But often before you can do this you need to learn to say 'no' to anything or anyone that drains your energy and is not in your best interests.

In this busy world, where we're all encouraged to be upbeat and positive and to say 'yes' to life, many of us find it extremely difficult to say 'no'. If you're someone who is always chasing around after others, it's highly likely that you need to learn to say 'no' a lot more than you currently do. If something isn't enhancing your life, ask yourself why you're doing it. Is it worthwhile? Has it outlived its purpose in your life? If you don't have a very good reason for something, just say 'no' to it!

If you find it difficult, practise. Stand in front of a mirror and let your mouth form the word 'no'. Next time you're faced with a request, buy yourself time by saying, 'Can I think about it?'

Someone once said to me, 'If you never say "no", then what is your "yes" worth?' If you think about this for a minute, by saying 'no', what you are doing is creating the space for your 'yes' to really mean something.

☆ *Saying 'Yes' and 'No' clearly builds confidence and rids us of the misconception that we are powerless.* ☆

Marsha Sintar

Make the things you say 'yes' to those that you can give your all to – those times when you can really help someone or those things that give you and others a great deal of pleasure. Let someone else do whatever it is you really want to say 'no' to!

☆ List your top 10 'no's – things you will eliminate from your life in order to ease your transformation. 'I will no longer … '

 5 Build Reserves to Conserve Time and Energy

Are you constantly dashing around trying to adhere to unrealistic deadlines? There's nothing worse than putting yourself under pressure, letting the adrenaline pump through your body when you make promises you know you're going to struggle to meet. Remember to build in a buffer – having reserves of time enables you to operate at your best, with less stress. If you arrive at appointments five or 10 minutes ahead of schedule, for example, you have time to get your thoughts together and make the most of the meeting.

As well as time reserves, build up physical reserves of commodities you use often. Not only does this save you the time and hassle of regular shopping trips, but also physical stocks of things are a constant reminder to you that you have established substantial reserves in your life and have more than enough to help your life flow easily. (Examples of this might be stocks of stationery, toilet paper, wine, or anything else that supports your lifestyle.)

Another secret of managing your time is to manage other people's expectations and 'under-promise and over-deliver'. By this I mean promising someone less than you know you can deliver. This relieves the pressure on you and helps you to optimize your time. When a person expects less and then receives more, they see you as very efficient and you become very attractive to them.

☆ What can you do to build in reserves of time in your life?

 ## 6 Energy Boosters

Once your energy blocks, niggles, limiting beliefs and clutter have been taken care of, you'll find you've created more space in your life for positive energy. What can you do to get more of this? Consider the following questions:

☆ Who and what gives you mental and emotional energy, inspiration and zest for life?

☆ What specific changes can you make to your health and wellbeing to increase your physical energy?

☆ Take action to integrate these energy boosters into your day-to-day life!

Remember, to change your life you need to change your approach and motivate yourself on your own terms. What works for you as an individual may not work for someone else. The more you understand yourself, the greater the likelihood of overcoming your resistance to blocks in your life.

Think back to a time when you felt motivated and in charge. What was happening around you? Connect regularly to your own source of motivation and you'll maintain the momentum to blast through any blocks!

☆ *Freedom is what you do with what's been done to you.* ☆

Jean-Paul Sartre

 7 Be Present in the Moment

Become more present in each moment. Give yourself time to slow down, notice all the details of your day-to-day life and take advantage of the external and internal cues around you. As you pay more attention to your world and adopt an open, receptive state of mind, you'll start to see more and to increase your awareness of flow. This is a time for inspiration and gaining new insights and fresh perspectives on things. When you're caught up in a fast-paced goal-driven life, you can fall into the trap of living in the future and overlooking the magic of the present. But when you pay attention to the moment, you'll probably be pleasantly surprised by the great opportunities that are staring you in the face, simply waiting to be noticed!

Being present in the moment sets you up to take full advantage of unforeseen circumstances. When things happen unexpectedly or you get a different outcome from the one you had originally hoped for, if you're paying attention, you can let the unexpected guide you to a new and perhaps better future. When your life is truly flowing and you allow yourself to be open-minded and let things fall into place naturally, your future can move towards you more quickly than you originally thought possible.

☆ How much of your time and/or energy is being lived (consciously or unconsciously) in or for the future instead of for today?

☆ What changes do you still need to make to ensure you're able to keep yourself focused and centred in the present moment?

Follow the Path of Least Resistance

Once you tap into the flow, you no longer need to push yourself hard to achieve the things you want in your life. Life can become easier and less of a struggle. Think of it like riding a bike. You've spent time and energy planning your route and have ridden up hill and down dale and now is the time to let go, freewheel down the hill and enjoy the ride!

☆ *When one door closes another one opens; but we often look so long and regretfully upon the closed door, that we do not see the ones which open for us.* ☆

Alexander Graham Bell

Quick Tip

'Don't should on yourself.'

In essence, if you say you 'should' or 'ought to' do something, unless you know it's something you genuinely *need* to do, the chances are the statement is coming from someone else's agenda and not from your own.

Be aware in your day-to-day life of how many times you say 'I should do this' or 'I should do that' – for example, do you ever say to yourself 'I should lose weight' or 'I should change jobs'? Stop and think. Ask yourself: 'Is this something I genuinely need or want to do?' I'm not suggesting you abdicate responsibility for things that it is necessary for you to do. We all have things in life that we don't particularly enjoy doing (housework or paperwork, for example), but we know we need to get them done. These are basic needs that you knuckle down and get on with. Equally, you may be required to take care of the needs of someone else (a sick relative perhaps), which is a question of facing up to your responsibilities.

From a realistic viewpoint, I'd like you to be aware of your needs, responsibilities and wants and make choices accordingly. If your 'should' is neither a need nor a genuine responsibility nor a want, I suggest it is not a true expression of yourself and not appropriate for you to do!

☆ Be aware of your language over the next few days and take note of how many times you say 'should' and 'ought'. List your 10 most common 'shoulds' and 'oughts', decide whether they are things you genuinely need or want to do and if they are not, consider what you are going to do about them.

I actively encourage you to connect as much as you can with the real reasons why you do things. If something doesn't feel right to you, don't do it. For example, if you find yourself working extra hours each week, ask yourself, 'Is there a good reason for this? How is it serving me?' If the answer is that this is something you need to do, because you're being paid overtime and you need the extra money perhaps, or the project is important to you, your company, client or customer, and you will all benefit, then the justification is there. However, if the real reason you're working longer is because you feel you 'should' because everyone else does or you've just got into the habit, stop and ask yourself whether you can do this differently. Are you 'shoulding' on yourself? Would it serve you better to develop ways of becoming more effective and productive in fewer hours?

Your life will become more fulfilling when you eliminate any sense of obligation to things that don't really serve you. Do the things you want to for your highest good – it's your life!

8 Learn from your Past

When you fully spring clean your life, an important area to address is that of issues from the past, especially those left over from any difficult times. As we grow and experience life, we all have our fair share of these and it may be during our darkest moments that we learn some of our most valuable lessons. But sometimes issues from the past hang around and become recurring patterns. In order to move on, you need to do something about them! Clearing up old issues and learning from past mistakes or disappointments can give you much firmer foundations for your future.

☆ What has your attention been drawn to during the more difficult periods of your life?

☆ What are the hardest lessons you've had to learn?

☆ Is there a problem or theme that rears its head time and time again?

☆ If you keep repeating the same pattern, why do you think this is so?

☆ Do you care enough about it to do something about it once and for all? If so, what will you do?

9 **Learn from your Problems**

It's not uncommon to find the problems or difficulties we encounter in life often, in hindsight, become our greatest gifts. They may not appear so at the time, but a very useful question to ask yourself is:

☆ What three key lessons am I learning from this experience that would make the biggest difference to me if I took action on them moving forwards?

Don't forget, learning is a life-long process, so put your heart into it, do the best you can in the circumstances, learn from your mistakes and tweak things as you go along.

☆ *Only those who will risk going too far can possibly find out how far one can go.* ☆

T. S. Eliot

☆ *Freedom lies in being bold.* ☆

Robert Frost

⭐5 boost
your
confidence

☆ *know your strengths and*
see things in perspective ☆

Overview

A key part of your life transformation is understanding and connecting with your own true self, valuing yourself for who you are and having the confidence to be the person you really want to be, optimising the contribution you can make to others.

Do you know what your genuine strengths are and how others really perceive you? Are you fully aware of the impact you have on others and what they appreciate you for?

In this chapter I want to help you to identify the seeds of your potential and to explore ways of nurturing them until they grow and come into full bloom. I want you to be naturally confident, happy and successful and still be true to yourself.

When you've completed this section:

☆ You'll be clear about your key strengths and how others view you
☆ You'll have created a clearer picture of WHO you want to be
☆ You'll start to focus your activities around what makes you unique and in the areas where you truly add value to others
☆ You'll be spending more time doing the things you enjoy and feel passionate about
☆ You'll be able to stand back and release pressure on yourself by seeing things in perspective
☆ You'll be exercising your 'confidence muscles' on a regular basis by maintaining a weekly confidence journal.

Quick Transformation Quiz

Answer the questions below by ticking the appropriate box and calculating your score as follows: 2 points = Yes/Agree/Not Applicable, 1 point = Agree sometimes, 0 point = No/Disagree

	YES	SOMETIMES	NO
1. I know what my key strengths are.	❏	❏	❏
2. I know what I'm passionate about and what inspires me.	❏	❏	❏
3. I understand the qualities that people appreciate in me and use them to help others.	❏	❏	❏
4. I understand what's unique about me and where I add value to others and consistently build on these characteristics.	❏	❏	❏
5. I build on my personal strengths and delegate my weaknesses to others.	❏	❏	❏
6. I believe in myself and my abilities and have a deep inner confidence and strong self-belief.	❏	❏	❏
7. I am expert at what I do and carry out my job better than most people I know.	❏	❏	❏
8. I look forward to going to work and/or my daily life.	❏	❏	❏
9. I rarely feel drained by the way I spend my day – essentially I have as much energy at the end of the day as I did at the start.	❏	❏	❏
10. I feel comfortable and able to fully express myself in the work I do and in the way I spend my time.	❏	❏	❏

Becoming the Person you Want to Be

Often the only thing that stops you from becoming the person you want to be is yourself and your own confidence. We limit ourselves from taking advantage of opportunities and achieving what's possible due to a lack of self-confidence. Are you as confident as you'd like to be? The chances are you're probably not. Success in life relies on having the confidence in your own capacity to make a difference and in your ability to succeed. It is also important to have the confidence to believe that your own experience, ambitions, needs and wants do really matter.

I believe you have the ability to become more confident and to develop into the person you want to be, if you pay attention to yourself and open yourself up to learn and grow. Self-confidence can be improved by working on the inside and strengthening your beliefs and inner sense of self and can also be developed externally by paying attention to your image, behaviour and how you project yourself in your outer world. One of the secrets to great self-confidence is to work on the internal and external elements simultaneously as one affects the other and vice versa. If you look confident but don't feel it, people will pick this up either consciously or subconsciously and the reverse is also often true.

Working from the inside out, it probably goes without saying that the better you get to know yourself, the more natural confidence you'll have! Understanding your strengths, roles, values and purpose will help you to connect with your own true essence and enable you to express yourself more confidently in the world. Taking time out to understand these key elements about yourself will set you in good stead for the rest of your life. Confidence is increased when you focus on what's working in your life and what you're good at, rather than what you're afraid isn't working. Focus on the positive and try to steer yourself away from negativity, problems and fears.

From an outward point of view improving your image and appearance and developing a confident body posture, behaviour, tone of voice and physiology can make you look and feel confident.

☆ Do you need a haircut?
☆ Would you benefit from a new skincare and make-up routine?
☆ Could you improve your posture?
☆ Do you maintain good eye contact with people?
☆ Do you smile with your eyes when you connect with people?
☆ Do you listen more than you talk?
☆ Would voice training help you?
☆ Do you dress appropriately?

Connect with your Strengths

We all have our own special gifts and the more we use them, the more we enhance our own lives, as well as those of people around us. So often, though, we take ourselves for granted and forget what makes us special. If I were to ask you to list out your strengths and to tell me what makes you sparkle, could you answer me directly? The chances are you find it easier to list your weaknesses than your strengths. Are you hiding your light under a bushel?

As your coach I want to ensure that you connect with your true essence as much as you can in your daily life. If you're playing to your strengths and expressing your true self, you're more likely to be enjoying yourself, feeling confident in your abilities and being appreciated by others in the process.

Your next step is to clarify what your strengths, abilities and natural gifts are. Find time over the next few days to sit quietly and complete the following exercises. You may well feel a little reluctant about doing them, but please give them a go, as when you've completed this step you'll have a much stronger sense of your own self.

Connecting with Yourself

☆ What are you brilliant at? Where do you excel? Make a list of all your *strengths* under the following categories:

> ☆ Physical
> ☆ Intellectual
> ☆ Social/Relationships
> ☆ Business/Financial
> ☆ Other

☆ Next, make a list of all your *weaknesses* in the same categories:

> ☆ Physical
> ☆ Intellectual
> ☆ Social/Relationships
> ☆ Business/Financial
> ☆ Other

☆ Now make a list of the things you *enjoy* doing in the same categories:

> ☆ Physical
> ☆ Intellectual
> ☆ Social/Relationships
> ☆ Business/Financial
> ☆ Other

☆ Finally make a list of the things you *don't* enjoy doing:

> ☆ Physical
> ☆ Intellectual
> ☆ Social/Relationships
> ☆ Business/Financial
> ☆ Other

☆ What insights can you draw from your own responses to these exercises?

Quick Tip

Trust your Intuition

Inner confidence and faith in yourself are valuable qualities and the more you can access them, the more readily you'll be able to manage the changes in your life. You can develop more of these characteristics if you pay attention to yourself and become more aware of your inner wisdom. I want you to make your intuition your ally, trust yourself and go with your 'gut' feelings.

How does your intuition speak to you? Do you receive information in words, do you get insights coming into your head or feelings in your body? If you're unfamiliar with accessing your intuition, ask yourself where you feel things in your body. If you have a decision to make, sit quietly and see where you feel something. The chances are you probably feel 'excitement' in one part of your body (maybe a fluttering sensation in your stomach, for example) and fear or foreboding in another area (your throat drying up perhaps?). You can use these feelings to interpret what your intuition is trying to tell you. Create the time and space to access your inner depths, be patient and allow yourself to discover your own answers when the time is right for you. Ask your intuition questions and pay attention to the answers. These might come to you as a quick flash of inspiration, an insight in a dream, a sense of 'knowing' in the pit of your stomach or perhaps a well-timed coincidence that endorses your own thoughts or makes sense to you in some way.

As your coach I want you to learn how to 'get out of your own way', to develop the ability to get out of your head and into your heart so you connect with your own inner wisdom on a regular basis. Getting out of your own way means putting your ego to one side and getting in touch with your own truth.

Often transformation begins with faith rather than fact. You need to have faith to trust your body's instincts, your heart's intuition and your mind's ability to work things out. But as you learn to step aside from your ego and learn to be really yourself, you make more room for truth and happiness.

Start a Confidence Journal

A great tool to help you build your confidence is to start a Confidence Journal and to revisit it once every week to update your thoughts. I do mine at the beginning of each week and sometimes refer back to it during the week to strengthen my resolve, centre myself and stay true to who I am.

Your confidence journal is a place where you record your answers to the following strengthening questions about yourself and your life:

☆ What am I most happy about in my life currently? Why do these things make me happy?

☆ What am I most proud about in my life currently? Why do these things make me proud?

☆ What am I most excited about in my life currently? Why do these things make me excited?

☆ Who do I love and enjoy being with in my life currently?

☆ Who loves and appreciates me for who I am?

Find yourself a notebook and answer these confidence questions once a week for the next month. Give yourself 10 minutes each time and enjoy building your confidence.

4 Strengths Feedback from Others

Another great way of getting in touch with your strengths and natural abilities is to ask for feedback from people who know you, whom you trust, respect and like. Sometimes other people can see our true essence more clearly than we can ourselves.

Your next task is to select five people who know you, ideally from different areas in your life, e.g. a family member, work colleague, school friend or a social contact, and ask them to answer, as honestly as they can, the following set of questions about you. You may, understandably, feel a little daunted about tackling this, but I'd like you to stretch beyond your comfort zones and give it a go! Swallow your pride, take a deep breath and be willing to open yourself up to the wisdom of those closest to you. My clients often say this is one of the most useful assignments they've ever done. You can make it easier by explaining the context to people. You might want to meet up with a friend or phone them to ask them the questions and get their spontaneous replies or you could e-mail the questions and give people their own time and space to respond. Alternatively, you can make a game of it and gather together a group of friends and all share feedback on each other, so everyone benefits!

The questions to ask are:

☆ What is the first thing you think of when you think of me?

☆ What do you think is the most interesting thing about me?

☆ What do you think my greatest accomplishment is?

☆ What do you value most about me?

☆ What do you perceive to be my greatest strengths?

To obtain more lateral feedback on how others see you, a great question to ask them is: 'If I were to appear on the front cover of a magazine, what sort of publication do you think it would be and what would the article inside be about?'

Once you've received all the feedback, I'd like you to collate the information together and look at common themes.

☆ Are you starting to connect with your own source of strength? Are you doing the things that make you sparkle?

☆ What lessons have you learned from these exercises? Is there a difference between how other people see you and how you see yourself?

☆ How many of the opinions you received coincide with each other? What are people's general opinions of you?

☆ Is there anything that surprises you in the answers you've received?

☆ What are the key insights you've learned?

☆ What do you think your own true essence is?

☆ What three things will you do to act on what you've learned?

☆ What changes are you willing to make to play to your strengths?

☆ Who are the people you can turn to who will bolster your self-confidence? Who believes fully in your ability to achieve everything you dream of?

☆ *He who knows others is wise. He who knows himself is enlightened.* ☆

Lao Tzu

5 What will you do MORE/LESS of?

We often spend our time day-dreaming about what we would do 'if only we had the time/money'. As you work your way through the transformation process, and rid yourself of obstacles and energy drainers, revisit your own 'if onlys' and start making dreams into realities. Imagine that you have time to focus on what you're good at and answer the following questions:

☆ What will you do more of?

☆ What will you do less of?

☆ Is your life currently based around your strengths and abilities?

☆ *Your only obligation in any lifetime is to be true to yourself. Being true to anyone else or anything else ... is impossible.* ☆

Richard Bach

6 Understand your Unique Value

We all have certain areas in our lives where we excel and it's the combination of our strengths, personal attributes and special qualities that makes each of us unique. What are your key areas of expertise? Perhaps you're superb at organizing and planning, maybe your special gift is coming up with creative ideas, managing finances or solving complex problems. The key to success is to focus on your own special qualities.

☆ What are your top three unique qualities?

☆ What do you believe is the real value you bring to your personal life?

☆ What do you believe is the real value you bring to your professional life?

☆ To what degree are your current roles and your key activities focused around your unique value?

Score yourself out of 10, with 10 being totally focused on where you add value and 0 being not using your unique abilities at all :

☆ Personal life: 1 2 3 4 5 6 7 8 9 10

☆ Professional life: 1 2 3 4 5 6 7 8 9 10

☆ What changes are you willing to make to bring your scores nearer to 10?

Once you've clarified your unique value in your personal and professional life, ask yourself what percentage of your daily life is actually spent doing the activities you're brilliant at. Ideally I want you to spend 80 per cent of your time focusing on what you do best. Is this possible for you?

☆ *When I stand before God at the end of my life, I would hope that I would not have a single talent left, and could say, 'I used everything you gave me'.* ☆

Erma Bombeck

 ## Step Back and Gain Perspective

When you come across a sticky patch, one of the most valuable actions is to stand back and remind yourself of the bigger picture of what you're doing. Ask yourself the following questions:

☆ What were my original reasons (and real benefits to me) for doing this in the first place?

☆ If I were to fast-forward my life three years ahead and then look back on this moment, what advice would I give myself?

☆ What is the worst possible thing that could happen to me now? Is it really that bad?

8 Look Creatively at Setbacks

One of the top traits of successful business people is their ability to develop creative responses to setbacks and obstacles. A valuable role of a lifecoach is to help people see their situation in perspective and to remind them of what's possible, during good times and bad. Looking creatively at setbacks and turning obstacles or problems into opportunities becomes a skill that can dramatically change the quality of your life.

☆ *Surmounting difficulty is the crucible that forms character.* ☆

Anthony Robins

Ask yourself Empowering Questions

Whatever issues you face, you'll find your ability to deal with them is strengthened by asking yourself empowering questions. If you feel stuck and disheartened by things going wrong, asking yourself a dis-empowering question such as 'Why did this happen to me?' is unlikely to get you anywhere, other than enmeshed more deeply in disabling self-pity mode.

When things are going wrong, rather than focus on the negative, ask yourself 'What do I really, really want from this?' Be realistic about the situation, acknowledge and accept the problem for what it is, face into it fully, ascertain the facts, but rather than 'crying over spilt milk', focus your energy on creating a compelling vision for yourself, 'Given the current reality, how can I make the most of the situation? What would the best-possible outcome look like?' Ask yourself the question 'How do I choose to feel about this?' Many of us allow external circumstances and people to determine how we feel about things, when instead we can choose to take responsibility for our own feelings and reactions. Taking back control over your feelings gives you a confidence in living that is priceless – you – and only you – can choose how you respond.

☆ 'If I knew I couldn't fail, what would I do about this situation?' When you focus on a successful outcome, it's amazing how your mind opens up to new possibilities and is willing to contemplate strategies that previously a 'more negative you' would never have allowed yourself to consider!

 Tap into your True Essence

By acknowledging your strengths and your weaknesses you stand in your own truth. Now I want you to make the most of your strengths and to delegate your weaknesses. Can you say 'no' to tasks that don't play to your strengths? Remember, success is about knowing who you are and what you enjoy and feel passionate about and taking action and doing it! When you can tap into your creativity and use your skills and strengths in your home and work, you'll be well on your way to a fulfilling life! Give yourself the freedom to express your true self and please hold on to this thought as you work through your next transformation steps.

☆ What will you do differently now to ensure you fully value yourself?

☆ *Nobody can make you feel inferior without your consent.* ☆

Eleanor Roosevelt

6 strengthen
your
relationships

*☆ create ongoing positive relationships
with yourself and others ☆*

Overview

The quality of our relationships often determines the quality of our lives. At the end of your life it's unlikely you'll be thinking about how hard you've worked, or how much money you've earned. True happiness is not based on your possessions, your power or your image, but on the quality of your relationships with people you love and respect.

I want you to create fulfilling one-to-one connections and a vibrant network of great people who will nurture and sustain you as you create the next phase of your life. I want you to surround yourself with people who can expand your horizons and help you to be more of who you are.

The assignments in this section will enable you to enhance your life by strengthening your relationships which, in turn, will help to propel you forwards towards your vision and the life you want.

When you've completed this section:

☆ You'll be clear about the relationships you want in your life
☆ You'll learn to give unconditionally and know what you can do to best serve others
☆ You'll start to acknowledge and appreciate others
☆ You'll start to clearly articulate what you need and want from others to be your best
☆ You'll have learnt how to improve your communication and relating skills so you start to attract and maintain more enriching, synergistic relationships into your life.

Quick Transformation Quiz

Answer the questions below by ticking the appropriate box and calculating your score as follows: 2 points = Yes/Agree/Not Applicable, 1 point = Agree sometimes, 0 point = No/Disagree

	YES	SOMETIMES	NO
1. I feel a special connection with key people in my life.		✓	
2. The people around me inspire me and make me feel good almost all of the time.			✓
3. I express myself fully; my true essence, spirit, love and vitality for life come across in the way I communicate with others.			✓
4. People enjoy my company; I tend to be light-hearted and good fun to be around.			✓
5. I am not afraid of being true to myself or appearing vulnerable in front of other people.			✓
6. I am kind and generous to others and am openly willing to share and to give.	✓		
7. I openly acknowledge people for who they are; I respect others and take an interest in their lives.	✓		
8. I listen carefully and hear what people are telling me and enable them to feel completely understood.		✓	
9. I speak clearly and warmly, am unconditionally constructive, encouraging and consistent in my support and reinforce the positive in others.	✓		
10. I am willing to love and to give love unconditionally without expecting anything specific in return.		✓	

Personal Relationships

Attraction and communication flow from who you are and how you live your life. People want to be with people whom they can trust, respect, relate to and like. One of the key lessons of attraction is that you attract who and what you are ready for in life. What you give out tends to get reflected back to you by those around you. For example, if you're feeling negative and critical about people, it's highly likely that the people in your life will be negative and critical towards you.

☆ *To laugh often and much; to win the respect of intelligent people and the affection of children; to earn the appreciation of honest criticism and endure the betrayal of false friends; to appreciate beauty and find the best in others; to leave the world a bit better; ... to know even one life has breathed easier because you have lived – this is to have succeeded.* ☆

Ralph Waldo Emerson

☆ Who are you attracting in your life now? What are the common themes and characteristics in your relationships?

Now you've established where you are with the relationships in your life, I would like you to clarify who you want to share the next phase of your life with.

Which people do you want to include in your life? What personal qualities are you looking for and what kind of interactions do you want to have?

☆ Who do you want to attract into your personal life? List the types of relationships, roles and interactions you're looking for (whether that's a significant other or relationships with friends and family).

☆ Of the relationships and qualities you've listed, which ones do you already have in your life now?

☆ What relationships or qualities and characteristics are currently missing in your life?

 Professional Relationships

Now turn your attention towards the workplace and the kind of relationships you need there in order to fulfil your goals.

☆ From a business/career point of view, what relationships and interactions would you like?

☆ Of the relationships and qualities you've listed, which ones do you already have in your life now?

☆ What relationships or qualities and characteristics are currently missing in your life?

I think it's important to point out here that whilst I've asked you to think about what your ideal relationships would look like, you will not necessarily find *all* your ideal qualities in one person. No one and nothing is perfect all of the time. If you can attract relationships that are 80 per cent of your ideal, you'll be well on your way to creating a happy and fulfilling life for yourself. If you can accept – or perhaps even enjoy – some imperfections in a relationship, your life will be enriched in the process.

Quick Tip

'Become your Own Best Friend'

If you want to build significant relationships in your life, whether with a loved one, friends, family, a client or colleague, it's important to address and strengthen your relationship with yourself first. The more you believe in yourself and respect yourself, the more others will believe in and respect you. The more attractive you feel on the inside, the more this will be reflected on the outside and in the world around you. Before you look for the qualities you want in others, think about what you can do to adopt the desired qualities yourself. Remember to be your own best friend.

3 Learn to Give Unconditionally

Giving to others without expectation of anything in return is probably the single most important way to attract people and improve your relationships. The giving in itself will heighten your own sense of self-worth and satisfaction.

Think about your own strengths and how you can use those qualities to help others. How can you best support others? What can you give and what do they want? How, by helping others, can you reach your goals faster and more easily? Tapping in to the power of others can elevate your life. I want you to benefit from the cross-fertilization of ideas, experiences, knowledge and wisdom by first giving of yourself.

☆ What can you give to others and how can you best serve them? List three things you can do more of to give to others.

 4 Acknowledge Others and Show You Care

Acknowledging people and showing them you care and want a lot for them is an extremely empowering way to build relationships.

☆ Choose three of the most important people in your life and tell them what you love and appreciate about them the most.

I challenge you to acknowledge at least three people daily. Ways of doing this could be sending them a card or 'Thank you' note, spending quality time with them, speaking with them on the telephone, sending them an e-mail, doing something (however small) you know they'll appreciate or arranging an activity to enjoy together.

 ## 5 Ask for What You Want

Don't be afraid to state clearly what you want in a relationship. A common mistake is to expect others to know what you need and want, which is often not the case. When you're able to ask for what you want, you become easier to be with, easier to please and much more attractive. People see you as clear and straightforward. I want you to learn how to ask for what you want in all your relationships. Tell people how they can be ideal for you – it will benefit you *and* them!

 ## 6 Address Problems Immediately

Don't overlook problems or bury issues or misunderstandings. Address them immediately. Don't deny, try to justify or blame someone else for a difficult situation, but realize you have the power to change it. Whatever the situation, you can take charge and manoeuvre the relationship onto a higher, more positive plane. Allow yourself to see an upset as an opportunity to learn something, change something or improve matters to everyone's advantage. Are there any outstanding issues or misunderstandings in your current relationships that need to be addressed? What are you willing to do about them?

7 Understand that People's Perceptions Become their Reality

The challenge in communication is that everyone has a different hold on reality based on their own perspectives, information and perceptions. I want you to accept that people are more than just their behaviour. The more you allow yourself to see things from a different perspective and realize that people do the best they can with the resources they have at hand, no matter how you look at a situation there are always two sides. Allow yourself to become more aware, over the next 10 days, of other people's perceptions. How can you use these insights to strengthen your relationships?

8 Put Yourself in their Shoes

Do your best to understand another person first before expressing your own point of view. Don't prejudge them or jump to conclusions. Ask clear questions and listen fully to the answers. The higher the quality of your questions, the easier it is to understand the answers. Listen with great empathy. Treat people with respect and respond to their needs. Put yourself in their shoes and seek to understand where they're coming from.

Then, from their perspective, think about the result that would constitute a win for you.

9 Become a Model of Who You Seek

If you're serious about improving your communication skills, look for role models and see what you can learn from them. Good communicators tend to have a 'lightness', clarity and well-developed sense of humour. The more you associate with these people, the greater the likelihood that their own characteristics will rub off on you! Remember, like attracts like, so become a model of what you seek. If you want more trust in your life, start by trusting yourself more. If you want more love, love yourself and others more – the chances are that love will be returned to you. Who are the people with successful relationships in your life? What can you learn from them?

☆ What characteristics do you appreciate in other people?

Reading through the qualities you've just written down, score yourself out of 10 for each. Give yourself 10 if you feel you're fully expressing this characteristic in your own life at the moment and only 1 if this is a quality you currently don't possess. It's easier to attract people with specific qualities if you already have them yourself. Think about what characteristics you want to develop in yourself now. Remember, awareness is the starting point, but action is key! Treat those you meet in the way you want to be treated yourself and this will be reflected back to you.

☆ *The most profound relationship we'll ever have is the one with ourselves.* ☆

Shirley Maclaine

☆ *The minute you begin to do what you want to do, it's a different kind of life.* ☆

Buckminster Fuller

☆7 tackle
your
obstacles

☆ *understand your blocks
and take action to
move forward* ☆

Overview

Do you sometimes find yourself full of plans of what you want and need to do, yet get frustrated with yourself by your apparent inability to take action, move forward and make them happen?

If you do, you're not alone – at some stage or another – we sabotage our own greatness and prevent ourselves from doing what we know we're capable of. We shoot ourselves in the foot time and time again and prevent ourselves from realising our true potential – WHY?

In this chapter we'll be exploring the secrets to sticking to your goals and making them happen. Understanding yourself and acknowledging what you're doing is the starting point, then there are a variety of positive steps you can take to move forward. I want to support you in addressing and overcoming any obstacles that could disrupt the flow of your transformation one by one.

When you've completed this section:

☆ You'll have identified significant obstacles
☆ You'll be confronting any specific blocks or challenges
☆ You'll have started to overcome your limiting beliefs
☆ You'll be more aware of 'positive evidence' in your life
☆ You'll be reminding yourself of success strategies that have worked for you in the past and will be applying them to present challenges
☆ You'll be closing any 'gaps' you have by taking action to develop new abilities and learn new skills.

Quick Transformation Quiz

Answer the questions below by ticking the appropriate box and calculating your score as follows: 2 points = Yes/Agree/Not Applicable, 1 point = Agree sometimes, 0 point = No/Disagree

YES SOMETIMES NO

1. I know what's important to me and have a strong sense of my direction in life.

2. I clearly understand which obstacles are holding me back.

3. I am aware of any limiting beliefs that are holding me back and am taking action to resolve them.

4. I have created some empowering beliefs which I remind myself of regularly, so I move forwards.

5. I actively look for evidence of positive things in my life, remember them often and build around them.

6. I know which success strategies work for me and use them to make my life easier.

7. I have a sense of inner peace and calm.

8. I am not afraid or worried about the future but am open to the experiences it brings.

9. I recognise that life is a journey and am constantly learning new skills and developing my abilities.

10. I am not afraid to ask for help and support when needed.

☆ *The real voyage of discovery consists not in seeking new landscapes, but in having new eyes.* ☆

Marcel Proust

 Significant Obstacles

Take a look back at Chapter Two when you were clarifying your visions and goals. The chances are you probably have a few obstacles blocking the way between where you are now and where you want to be. Once you become more aware of these, you can start to develop ways of overcoming them.

The obstacles can either be internal or external. Internal obstacles are thoughts, feelings and ways of behaving that prevent you from reaching your full potential. External obstacles are outside issues that have an impact on your life. Take a look at the following threats and tick the ones that are likely to influence you or become an obstacle to your success:

Internal	External
Negative habits/attitudes	Money
Procrastination	Loss of your job
Fear	Divorce
Low self-confidence	Recession
Perfectionism	Ageing parents
Failure	Dysfunctional family

Stress

Poor time management

Loneliness

Resistance to change

Limiting self-beliefs

Fear of success

Depression

Hopelessness

Inflation

TV and media

Ageism

Addictions

Political change

Racism

Sexism

 Personal Obstacles

Some of the obstacles in our lives are not real but imagined. Often, understanding exactly what stops us from achieving is the first step towards starting to achieve! In order to move towards your personal goals write down each goal and then answer the following questions.

☆ What blocks or challenges could prevent you from achieving each personal goal?

☆ What will you do to overcome the obstacle or block? Do you need to develop any new skills or get someone to help you?

Quick Tip

Act as if Success is Already Yours

A quick tip for moving through obstacles speedily is to hold your chin up, stand up straight, shoulders tall and act as if you've ALREADY achieved what it is you seek. Do NOT allow yourself to look down and get swamped by self-doubt. Even if you do not feel very confident now, acting as though you are already achieving what you want will propel you forwards in life. You'll be surprised how your confidence catches up with you and your obstacles disappear!

 Professional Obstacles

Now look at your professional life.

☆ What blocks or challenges could prevent you from achieving each professional goal?

☆ What will you do to overcome the obstacle or block? Do you need to develop any new skills or get someone to help you?

4 Limiting Beliefs that Hold You Back

We wouldn't be human if we didn't hold beliefs. Many are ingrained in us from a young age and become our reality without us even realizing it. Beliefs such as 'Life is a struggle' and 'You have to work hard to earn money' are very common.

If you're finding it difficult to make the progress you want, the chances are it is probably your beliefs that are holding you back in some way. They may be negative phrases you often find yourself repeating in your head. Time and again in my lifecoaching sessions I come across a whole series of limiting beliefs such as 'I'm not good enough', 'Things like that don't happen to me', 'I'm too short/fat/stupid to succeed', 'I don't have the right skills for that role', 'My boss knows best', etc.

If you want to transform your life, becoming aware of the beliefs you hold is an important start. Understanding why you hold such beliefs and acknowledging the evidence that supports them is the second stage. The next step is about turning limiting beliefs into empowering ones. Stage four is about finding the evidence to support the empowering beliefs. The final step involves implementing the empowering beliefs into your everyday life.

☆ What are your limiting beliefs?

☆ Which one do you think has the most influence over you?

☆ Why do you hold this belief? What evidence do you have to prove that it is true?

☆ What evidence do you have to prove to yourself that this belief is not *necessarily* true?

5 Empowering Beliefs to Move You Forwards

☆ Having looked at your existing belief patterns:

> ☆ What would be a more positive, empowering belief that could replace your old belief?
> ☆ What evidence do you have to support your new empowering belief?
> ☆ What are you willing to do differently to integrate this new empowering belief into your life transformation?
> ☆ What has to happen for you to feel in charge and able to overcome any blocks or limiting beliefs?

6 Success Strategies that Work for You

☆ Think back to a time when you were previously successful and effectively overcame any obstacles in your path. Write down three key things you did that helped you. Can you apply them to your current circumstances? What are your next steps to overcome each obstacle?

Tools that Help

☆ Think back to Chapter Three when you identified resources that would support you. Are any of these relevant to overcoming these obstacles? If not, sit down and write a list of any resources that would help you right now, whether it's a mobile phone, a particular book or even an effective filing system so that everything is in easy reach.

 Developing New Skills

If training would help you overcome any obstacles at the moment, whether in your personal or professional life, take some time and write a list of what added training or skills you need. Then look on the Internet or go to the library and find the appropriate course. So whether it's learning book-keeping, learning to drive or taking up yoga in order to destress, find out more.

 Getting Others to Help You

In Chapter Three, I stressed the importance of surrounding yourself with key people to support you and to hold you accountable for your actions. I trust that you're already benefiting from their help? There are undoubtedly times in your life when it's useful to spend time alone and to work things through for yourself. However, no matter how self-sufficient you are, there are also many occasions when your life can be significantly enhanced by the support of others.

Surround yourself with people who can help you take your life onto the next level – both an 'inner' and an 'outer' team. 'Inner' team members are a few key people you have relatively close contact with, see and speak to regularly and know are consistently there for you. Your 'outer' team members are those people who are more on the periphery of your life. You don't necessarily have direct access to them – they can be role models you admire from afar or useful contacts you touch base with every once in a while.

Can you identify the key people in your network who can help? Are you making the most of your relationships with them? How can they help you tackle your obstacles? Who are the top three people in your wider environment who inspire and motivate you? Are you spending sufficient time with them? They could help catapult you to the top of your field!

☆   My top three catapults are:

☆ *Without continuous personal development you are now all that you will ever become, and hell starts when the person you are meets the person you could have been.* ☆

Eli Cohen

8 gain focus and achieve more in less time

☆ plan ahead, clarify your priorities and stay focused ☆

Overview

Time is one of the most valuable gifts you can give anyone – including yourself! We're all so busy these days that the ability to make the best use of time is an important factor in determining our happiness and success.

A cornerstone in transforming your life is planning ahead and focusing on your priorities. You'll find it difficult to achieve your goals unless you're managing your time effectively. The assignments in this section will enable you to focus and manage yourself so you achieve more in less time.

In effect managing time is more to do with how we manage ourselves than anything else. We can't control time but we can control ourselves. We all have the same 24 hours in each day – I want you to get the most out of yours. The more effective use you make of your time, the quicker you'll see your life transform!

I want you to get time on your side so you derive greater satisfaction – and less stress - from the results you want to achieve!

When you've completed this section:

☆ You'll be taking the time to plan and will have set up an effective time management system for yourself
☆ You'll have clarified your priorities and will be investing time wisely
☆ You'll have identified three priorities for the next three months
☆ You'll have identified three priorities for the month ahead
☆ You'll be using the power of daily focus, every day of your life
☆ You'll be managing time on your terms, having eliminated time wasters and built reserves. You'll be monitoring and evaluating your performance regularly so you consistently achieve more in less time.

Quick Transformation Quiz

Answer the questions below by ticking the appropriate box and calculating your score as follows: 2 points = Yes/Agree/Not Applicable, 1 point = Agree sometimes, 0 point = No/Disagree

	YES	SOMETIMES	NO
1. I have plenty of time to do the things I want to do.	❏	❏	❏
2. I am realistic about how I spend my time and about the length of time it takes to accomplish specific tasks.	❏	❏	❏
3. I identify my key priorities on an ongoing basis.	❏	❏	❏
4. At any one moment I am clear about what is the single most important investment in my time.	❏	❏	❏
5. I make time daily to plan.	❏	❏	❏
6. I commit to deadlines and consistently deliver on time.	❏	❏	❏
7. I rarely procrastinate but maintain myself in the flow.	❏	❏	❏
8. I am willing to say 'no' and am clear when to do a task myself or delegate it.	❏	❏	❏
9. I am continually innovating and improving the way I work and the things I do.	❏	❏	❏
10. I pace myself and honour my personal energy cycles.	❏	❏	❏

☆1 Clarify your Priorities

I'm sure that most of us will acknowledge that the more we focus on the priorities in our life, the more quickly we are likely to achieve our desired outcomes. If you've already spring cleaned your life, removed many of the distracting obstacles in your way and become clearer about your own strengths and values, you'll be ready to focus now on what's important. Remember, highly successful people are very focused – they recognize their priorities and strengths and delegate the rest. Focusing on priorities also helps you to avoid getting side-tracked by those unimportant yet urgent activities that can take over your day-to-day life, as no doubt you discovered in the time-tracking exercise! Make your time work for you by concentrating on the most important priorities, so you can achieve a lot more in less time.

Investing your Time Wisely: The 80/20 Rule

We all have the same 24 hours in a day but sometimes it doesn't feel like enough time. It's a fact of life that there is often more for you to do than you can possibly do in the time available. So you need to make wise choices about how you invest your time and energy. It's as important that you're doing the right things as much as you're doing things right!

I'd like you to think for a moment about the 80/20 rule. That is, 20 per cent of all your activities are likely to produce 80 per cent of the meaningful results in your life. Think for a minute. What is your 20 per cent? What is the small handful of activities that will really produce the key results in your life?

☆ What are the three things that will make the biggest difference to your life and work and move you towards your vision?

Once you've completed this exercise I'd like you to really think about the top 20 per cent as being your 'gold time' activities. The more time you spend working on these activities, the more quickly you'll see your life transforming. Make sure you make inroads into these tasks with every opportunity you get. At every odd moment try to keep doing things that move your gold activities along. Remember, don't procrastinate, do these activities now, don't waste time on non-focused activities.

Remember to make sure that your 'gold' focused time is spent doing what you genuinely do best. If you're unsure about this, go back to Chapter Five and reconnect with your strengths and your own value. Remember, the more you spend your time playing to your strengths, the more fulfilling it will be.

☆ *Imagination is the highest kite that one can fly.* ☆

Lauren Bacall

 2 Focus on the Power of Three

I want you to ensure you focus on no more than three important activities so you give them as much time as you can. This is often a huge challenge to many of my clients. It's very tempting to take on more. But if you're serious about making a success of your life, maintaining your focus is imperative. It requires self-discipline and the ability to say 'no'. Too many of us spend our time rushing around, chasing our tails, coping, solving problems and fire fighting. This is not what I want for you. When you lose sight of your key priorities, it's impossible for you to be effective.

☆ My Top Three Priorities for the Year Ahead
1.
2.
3.

 Three Priorities for Three Months

It is not uncommon to feel overwhelmed by the sheer magnitude of what needs to be done to transform your life so be more specific and take one step at a time. Focus on what you want to do in the next three months.

☆ My Top Three Priorities for the Next Three Months
1.
2.
3.

Now focus on what you want to achieve in the next month.

☆ My Top Three Priorities for the Next Month
   1.
   2.
   3.

You need to review your general priorities on a weekly and daily basis, but the importance of clarifying your priorities, tracking and monitoring them cannot be overemphasized. As you fill in these sections, think about your answer to the questions:

☆ If nothing else gets done this year, what would I be happy with achieving?

☆ If nothing else gets done in the next three months except x, what would that be?

 4 Daily Focus

Think about ways you can incorporate elements from each of your goals into your daily routine, so they become a natural part of your life. List them in your daily inspiration journal, read them every morning and evening and remember that as you repeat them in your subconscious mind, they'll become more embedded and more real.

☆ If I only achieve three things today, what do I want them to be?

☆ Allow 15 minutes at either the start or the end of each day to set your schedule for the day ahead, so you create a daily plan before you do anything else. Ask yourself, 'What is most important about today?' and make sure you prioritize this above everything else.

5 Taking on Too Much

Trying to do everything yourself can be a huge time waster. Taking on the whole world may feel heroic, but is highly unlikely to be in your best interests. Become a master of delegation! You've already done plenty of work on clarifying your strengths and priorities. Focus on these and delegate as much of the rest as you can.

It's a human tendency to lull ourselves into a false sense of security thinking that we are the only people who can do a specific job. It's easy to become reluctant to delegate any tasks to an assistant or to outsource it to someone else completely. Accept that even if the task isn't exactly up to your standards, as long as it's done well enough, let it be. Remember, you need to play to your strengths. If you're someone who has trouble handing work over to others, realize the benefits of paying someone else to do what you don't enjoy or what you're not good at. Whether that's paying someone to clean your house or taking on an extra member of staff to handle some of the routine tasks at work, do it!

☆ Make a list of the top 10 tasks that you can delegate, to whom you'll delegate them and when.

Quick Tip

Honour your Personal Energy Cycles

Are you a morning or an evening person? When is the best time of day for you to do specific activities? Are you best handling phone calls first thing in the morning or is the morning your best time for being quiet, writing and thinking, planning and developing? When is the best time of the day for you to be outgoing? When is it best for you to focus on concentrated activities?

Our personal energy cycles vary. If you become aware of yours, you can plan your days, weeks and months accordingly. You may well find your energy levels vary on different days in the week. Monday might be a good day for you to do administrative tasks and to be internally focused whereas a Friday might be a day for you to be out and about. Think about where different tasks can best be fitted into your day and build these in as part of your routine.

☆ What changes will you make to honour your own personal time and energy flows?

☆ What is the best use of your time right now?

☆ *The biggest human temptation is to settle for too little.* ☆

Thomas Merton

 ## 6 Take the Time to Plan

We all have 8,760 hours in our year, but it's our choice what we do with them. I encourage you to set up a clearly planned time management system tailor-made to your own needs and key activities.

The more you organize your time, the easier you'll find it to create space for spontaneity. It might seem somewhat of a paradox, but those who fail to plan and structure their time often find themselves more restricted, with less free time, than their well-organized counterparts!

If you're someone who resists using a time planner, the chances are you're likely to benefit from it most! Once you get into the habit of planning ahead, your life will flow more easily. I want you to set time aside regularly to plan your future and monitor your progress towards your goals. Use your diary or planner and block out specific personal and business planning time as follows:

Yearly Overview

Schedule in one day's 'personal think-tank time' every year to give you your annual focus for what you want to achieve in the coming year. This is often great to do at New Year or around your birthday, when you're likely to be more inclined to focus on your goals for the year ahead.

Also plan in your key tasks, holidays and special events, family occasions and regular meetings, so you can start to see how you want your year to look and the key results you want to achieve at specific times.

An Overview Every Three Months

It is useful to monitor your progress and track your goals every three months, so plan in three hours at a time to do this.

 Plan your Time in Blocks

Categorize your key activities and block out specific days or times in the week to do them. Planning your day in blocks and allocating specific lengths of time to certain activities will help to keep you focused and on track. Be realistic about how long things take and when your time is up on one activity, make sure you discipline yourself to move on to the next task. This way you will make measurable progress on each task and not let yourself get bogged down! If you're a visual person you might like to use a highlighter pen and colour in allocated blocks of time on your planner.

It's a fact of life that you'll get interruptions in your day-to-day life that you can't foresee. To some degree they may be out of your control. Allowing for contingency time is vital in helping you to keep control of your life. I want you to create space for the unexpected, so make sure that you allocate time in your daily schedule to handle interruptions and unscheduled events. Also, give yourself a few hours 'catch up' time every once in a while to deal with any backlog of tasks that may have built up. Provided you give yourself this extra buffer within your schedule, the chances are that you'll have the flexibility to handle more or less anything that's thrown at you!

 8 Procrastination Busters

Procrastination is the art of putting things off and many of us are extremely skilled at it! Are you someone who can be very creative in thinking up excuses? Putting things off and/or leaving them to the last minute can mean you waste a considerable amount of time and effort worrying about them, causing yourself stress and undermining your ability to take charge of your life. The only way to break out of this is to just get on and take action.

A great way of blasting through procrastination is to identify the most unpleasant job on your 'to do' list, and tackle it first, before you do anything else. Psychologically this will set you up for success – everything else will seem easy, once you've tackled the worst task! Alternatively, break a large onerous task down into small chunks and allocate, say, 15 minutes every day to chipping away at it steadily so you feel as though you're making progress effortlessly!

☆ What are you procrastinating about? List everything, select the worst item on your list and just do it!

☆ What three things can you stop doing this week that will stop you wasting your time?

9 Take Regular Breaks

Don't forget to block out time for yourself, where you simply relax and recharge your batteries. However busy you are, when you take regular time to withdraw and recharge you'll find it's easier to maintain high levels of efficiency, productivity and an inner sense of calm. Taking five-minute breaks regularly throughout the day, having a lunch break or time out sitting quietly, taking a walk, breathing deeply and feeling peaceful will increase your levels of concentration and your ability to achieve more in less time.

☆ *A dream is just a dream. A goal is a dream with a plan and a deadline.* ☆

Harvey Mackay

☆ *Let money work for you, and you have the most devoted servant in the world ... It works night and day, and in wet or dry weather.* ☆

P.T. Barnum

⭐9 shape up
your
finances

☆ *plug your money drains and create firm financial foundations* ☆

Overview

A fundamental part of transforming your life is establishing a firm financial platform from which to operate.

When your financial situation is in order it's much easier to be yourself – you tend to feel a lot healthier, you can lead a relatively stress-free life, are more relaxed and able to focus on your key life goals. In essence money provides you with the means and the energy to create your dreams.

As your coach, I want you to shape up your finances so they work for you, give you energy and support you. I want you to feel in control of your money and of your financial reserves and have a savings plan that makes you feel responsible, not just for now, but for the future.

Your financial situation says a lot more about you than your money. Your finances are often a litmus test of your own level of self worth and also give an indication of your willingness to invest in yourself as a person. If you want to live a fulfilling life, taking charge of your finances is crucial.

When you've completed this section:

☆ You'll have taken charge of your financial situation by eliminating debt and planning your expenditure
☆ You'll have plugged any drains on your money
☆ You'll be saving for your future
☆ You'll have established an effective financial support system
☆ You'll be acknowledging your beliefs and blocks about money and the impact they have on your life
☆ You'll be taking action towards improving your financial situation and opening yourself up to prosperity.

Quick Transformation Quiz

Answer the questions below by ticking the appropriate box and calculating your score as follows: 2 points = Yes/Agree/Not Applicable, 1 point = Agree sometimes, 0 point = No/Disagree

	YES	SOMETIMES	NO
1. I am totally honest with myself about my money situation.	❏	❏	❏
2. I know what my expenditure levels are and live on a weekly budget which allows me to save.	❏	❏	❏
3. I have repaid any borrowings or have a clear plan as to how I will repay any monies owing to others.	❏	❏	❏
4. I am currently saving a minimum of 10 per cent of my income.	❏	❏	❏
5. I understand my own beliefs about money and if any one of them is holding me back I am taking action to address it.	❏	❏	❏
6. I know I am earning what I deserve.	❏	❏	❏
7. I have a clear financial plan for the year ahead.	❏	❏	❏
8. I never feel held back by money or the lack of it.	❏	❏	❏
9. I have people around me who will support me with my financial plans.	❏	❏	❏
10. I feel relaxed about money and am ready and willing to open myself up to abundance.	❏	❏	❏

1 Take Charge of your Finances

I now want you to take full charge of shaping up your finances. Money worries can be a huge energy drain. It's virtually impossible to transform your life if you're being dragged down by financial insecurity and a negative cash flow. The sooner you can address these issues, the better!

Establish your Financial Reality

How honest are you with yourself about your financial situation? Are you totally clear about how much you spend, how much you earn, how much you save? Do you have a strategy in place to make yourself financially secure and independent?

Perhaps unsurprisingly, many of us dread knowing the truth about our financial situation. It's not uncommon to be vague about your expenses, about how much you spend and where your money goes at the end of the week or at the end of the month. In general we all spend at least 10 per cent more than we realize. Strengthening your financial situation is not necessarily as difficult as it may seem. The starting point is to clarify your current income and expenditure.

Take a look at your income pattern over the past year and work out what your average monthly income is. Does your income vary from month to month or is it relatively stable?

☆ My current average monthly income is £ ...

If you're not fully aware of the true extent of your monthly outgoings, take time to work them out. You may find it useful to track your actual expenditure over the next month. Be aware of both monthly bills and tiny daily expenses. Summarize them at the end of the month and see how much you really spend.

☆ My current average monthly expenditure is £ ...

 Eliminate Debt

The initial stage of the money merry-go-round is to get out of debt. If you have debts – credit card debts, loans, overdrafts and borrowings – take full responsibility for them and work at erasing them from your life. You might want to consolidate your debts, cut up your credit cards and check you're paying the lowest interest rates on outstanding loans.

☆ Some people find a great way of managing their expenditure is to cut up all their credit, debit and store cards and simply operate with cash. If you think this could work for you, why not spend the next three months operating on a cash-only basis. This will help you to keep track of exactly where you are and how much you're spending. If you draw a set amount of cash at the beginning of every week, your challenge is to live off that without extending yourself.

Quick Tip

Acknowledge Abundance

Many people build their lives on the principle of scarcity or lack, believing there is never enough to go round. This becomes a self-fulfilling prophecy as they go about their day-to-day lives struggling to make ends meet. Abundance and scarcity are both a matter of perception. Once you change your perception, feeling and action will follow.

I want you to come from a place of abundance. The starting-point for this is to appreciate how much abundance you already have in your life. In the Western world we live in a land of plenty – our homes are full of luxuries, clothes, furniture and equipment we rarely use, we are surrounded by friends and most of us enjoy lives of relative prosperity. Do you suffer from poverty consciousness? Do you hear yourself saying 'I can't afford that' or 'It's too expensive'? Beliefs of scarcity and lack are caused by social conditioning.

☆ What are the areas of lack or scarcity in your life? What are you willing to do about them?

Let go of any habits of poverty. Give your loose change to people in need and open yourself up to receiving positive energy in return.

Abundance is very much a state of being and a measure of the confidence you have about life. I want you to cultivate feelings of confidence and richness in your life on an ongoing basis. Recall a time in your past when you felt a deep sense of richness, remember how you felt and hold onto these feelings now. I want you to give off an air of abundance, then others will reflect this back to you.

3 Plug Money Drains

Having taken a look at your income and expenditure patterns and clarified where your money goes, I want you to look at ways in which you can reduce your monthly expenditure by between 10 and 30 per cent. It's not how much you earn that determines your financial situation, but how much you keep!

How can you trim back your expenditure? You might like to enlist the help of a friend to go through your expense records and see where you can cut back. If you both do the exercise at the same time, you can challenge each other to cut down. Why not have a reciprocal arrangement in which you help your friend to reduce their outgoings by 25 per cent and they help you to do yours?

☆   List at least five things that you can start doing to reduce your expenditure.

Many of us spend money on things that we don't really need. Think about money spent on sweets, magazines or any items that you don't use. Also consider whether you're paying too much for your insurance or the mortgage on your home. Maybe you could reduce the amount of tax you pay.

☆ Find 10 unrewarding ways that you spend your money.

Create a spending plan for yourself. Make it realistic. Record how much you actually spend against how much you plan to spend and look at the difference. Don't spend more than you make. Work with your plan for six months and then take a rain check and decide how you're progressing.

4 Start Saving for the Future

Financially successful people tend to save at least 20 per cent of their income. What are your savings plans? Have you looked at your pension recently? What does your investment portfolio look like?

Embarking on a major savings initiative might be too radical for you at the moment, but do *something* now, even if the step you take is a small one. If you begin saving an extra £5 per week and work up to 10 per cent of your income, this is a step towards success. Take it – you'll be glad you did.

☆ What actions will you take to start saving?
   You might need to use your own creativity for this and also brainstorm ideas with a friend, but if you simplify your lifestyle and also start to save, what you're doing is giving yourself freedom for the future. You're starting out on a track towards financial security and independence. Whether you save an additional £10, £100 or £200 a week, it is all an investment towards your future. Maintaining one month's living expenses in your current account and three months' expenses in a savings account will provide you with a good financial platform.

5 Set up a Financial Support System

As you start to cut down your expenditure, reduce your debts and develop savings plans, you may well find that you need to work with a friend who is good with money or a financial adviser.

To really set yourself up for financial success you may want to consider investing in a financial software package for your computer or changing your bank, employing a book-keeper, an accountant or a financial planner. If this is necessary, the first thing is to find someone you can trust.

 ## 6 Emotional Blocks about Money

Your relationship with money can tell you a lot about yourself. For example, if your money is out of control the chances are some part of your emotional life is also out of control. If you're stingy and tight with money it may well be that you're afraid of love and intimacy. If you're constantly worried about running out of money, perhaps you're afraid of being left alone. If you never have enough money, ask yourself whether it is because you believe that you are not worth enough. If you often say, 'I'm broke', do you actually feel broken or wounded inside for some reason?

If you're always borrowing money from other people, ask yourself whether you think you deserve more than you receive emotionally and whether you can get those emotional needs met elsewhere. If you find money slipping through your fingers and never feel as though you can have enough for yourself, is this perhaps because you don't think you deserve prosperity? If you need to be rescued financially, this may be an indication that you may be feeling needy, alone or unloved.

☆ Take 10 minutes to clarify the most significant emotional blocks you have about money.

 ## 7 What Holds You Back Financially?

Before you move on to setting your financial goals for the future, it's important to take a look at anything that might hold you back financially. You may have developed unhealthy money habits, think your finances are unimportant, hold limiting beliefs about your ability to earn money or not trust yourself to effectively manage your finances. Unless you address these issues, you'll find it very difficult to create future financial security.

☆ What mistakes do you repeatedly seem to make with money?

☆ What lessons have you learned in the past from your finances?

 ## 8 Create new Financial Truths

As your coach I want you to be very honest with yourself. If there's something that's holding you back on an emotional level it may well be that your money situation is a physical manifestation of it. At the end of the day, money is a reflection of the universal flow of energy in your life. If there are blocks at some level, the more you work to remove them, the more easily your life will flow.

☆ What new financial truths would you like to create for yourself about money?

 # 9 Five Actions to Improve your Finances

As your coach I want to help you move towards financial freedom, so you regularly gain enough income to more than meet your own needs. If you want to increase your income, why not think about your top five ways of earning more money? Do you need to update and refine your business or career plan? Do you need to do more training or learn new skills? In your current job, is it appropriate for you to ask for a pay rise? Move jobs if you need to and start to develop a plan to attract a higher-paying job before you leave.

☆ Make a list of things you could do to improve your financial situation, things which you would respect and admire yourself for.

Start doing them!

☆ *There is no end. There is no beginning. There is only the infinite passion of life.* ☆

Federico Fellini

10 take action, maintain
momentum
and flow

☆ *pay regular attention to your goals
and celebrate your successes* ☆

Overview

Congratulations on reaching this final section! By now your life transformation will be well underway – keep up the great work! I hope you've already enjoyed some fabulous wins and have surprised yourself with some of the things you've now achieved. We really are capable of so much more than we can currently conceive. As your pocket life coach draws to a close, I want you to suspend all disbelief and open your mind to your own limitless potential.

I know ordinary people can do extraordinary things. Time and time again I see my clients surprise themselves with some of the actions they find themselves taking! You can achieve anything you believe in, if you really put your mind to it. I want this final section to inspire you to open yourself up to capture that extra magical something in your life. As we finally pull the whole process together, you'll be inspired to step outside of your comfort zones, take advantage of synchronicity, celebrate your successes – big and small – and create real momentum to transform your life on an ongoing basis!

When you've completed this step:

☆ You'll be creating your vision on a daily basis
☆ You'll be anchoring your success with symbols and affirmations
☆ You'll be pacing yourself and accepting the ebbs and flows
☆ You'll have the courage to take risks
☆ You'll become more aware of synchronicity
☆ You'll be paying attention to the moment, recognizing opportunities and getting into the flow of your life.

Quick Transformation Quiz

Answer the questions below by ticking the appropriate box and calculating your score as follows: 2 points = Yes/Agree/Not Applicable, 1 point = Agree sometimes, 0 point = No/Disagree

	YES	SOMETIMES	NO
1. I am optimistic about myself and the future ahead of me.	❏	❏	❏
2. I am open and aware of the things going on around me and fully respond to them.	❏	❏	❏
3. I rarely get tired or become ill and am well connected to my own energy source.	❏	❏	❏
4. I am living my own life on my own terms and feel fully satisfied.	❏	❏	❏
5. I am open to synchronicity and to the remarkable people that come into my life.	❏	❏	❏
6. I am consistent. People understand me and know where they stand with me.	❏	❏	❏
7. I live a life of excellence and am constantly doing my best in everything I do.	❏	❏	❏
8. I am willing to take risks and to trust that what will be will be.			
9. I feel totally in the flow of life – it's fun and fulfilling and I'm engaged in creating a wonderful future.	❏	❏	❏
10. If I were to die today, it would be with few regrets.	❏	❏	❏

☆ *The next message you need is always right where you are.* ☆

Ram Das

 ## 1 Integrate Action into Your Daily Life

As your coach, I want you to get into the swing of maintaining your momentum and applying your new knowledge on an ongoing basis. Moving ahead one small step at a time and taking regular daily actions towards the future you want will create a natural momentum to propel you forwards. Keep your vision, intentions and goals in your daily sight, acknowledge them in written form in your planner and your daily inspiration journal, acknowledge them verbally in your affirmations and integrate them into your everyday life. Expand your knowledge by reading books on related topics, attending courses or workshops and learning more about whatever interests you.

 ## 2 Bring your Vision Alive Every Day

Paying regular attention to your goals will help speed up the transformational process. Look at your destiny map regularly and remind yourself of the big benefits of your goals every now and again. Remember, if you keep your goals realistic and SMART, 'what the mind can conceive, it can achieve'. Any goal that truly fires your imagination and fills your heart with joy is reachable. (Make sure you focus your attention on what you want in your life, and not on what you don't want, as putting your attention on the negative might bring it into being!)

Develop Affirmations

Why not use affirmations to support you in moving your goals forward? Affirmations expand your beliefs and stimulate your imagination. A great way of developing affirmations is to give yourself a series of positive present tense statements describing the benefits of your goal and how you'll feel when you reach it. Your statements can be short, but make them believable yet exciting. Either write them down or read them out or even record them onto a cassette for playing in your car or at home. If you say them aloud at bedtime, they're likely to enter your subconscious mind, which will assimilate them as reality while you sleep.

Act as if your Goal Already Exists

From the moment you're clear about your goals, I want you to start acting as if they are already in existence. If you act in a successful way from the very beginning you're much more likely to achieve the results you want. Don't wait for things to happen to you – the more you act as if they're here now, the sooner they'll come to you.

Quick Tip

'Make Fear your Friend'

When you start taking action, the secret is to keep moving. If you find yourself feeling stuck, ask yourself what it is that you're afraid of? Instead of turning away because you feel anxious, let your butterflies fly in formation. A fellow coach once said 'Fear is excitement without the oxygen'. Think what constitutes oxygen for you? How can you breathe, nurture yourself and give yourself courage to stretch beyond your comfort zones? Allow yourself to be comfortable with your 'fear', take a small action to stretch yourself to new heights and trust you'll get the support you need. No doubt you've heard the phrase 'feel the fear and do it anyway' – so how about it?

☆ What are you afraid of and what small action can you take today to face into it and move yourself forward, in even the smallest way?

 Anchor Your Success

You can maintain the momentum by choosing a symbol that you can see daily to remind you of your transformation. You might like to select an item of jewellery, an ornament or a picture that acts as a constant reminder to stay on track.

6 Accept the Ebbs and Flows

Whilst enjoying the natural momentum you're creating in your life, don't forget that there will be ebbs and flows. Tune into your inner wisdom and pace yourself in accordance with what feels right for you. The chances are you'll grow and evolve quickly on some occasions and more slowly on others. Give yourself time to absorb and assimilate what you've learned and don't push yourself to move too fast. Remember, you're likely to reach your results through a cycle of ups and downs.

We all go through 'challenging' patches every now and again. Let's face it – we are human! When you're in an inactive place, don't give up – it won't last forever. Sometimes it's during our apparently 'inactive' and 'ugly' phases that we're undergoing our most important learning experiences. Often nothing appears to be happening just before a major growth spurt. Think of a caterpillar becoming a rather ugly, inactive chrysalis before it bursts back into life as a beautiful butterfly. Accept that we must all go through a 'chrysalis' phase every once in a while! Find ways to enjoy your life, accept any lulls you may experience and maintain your focus on what you want.

7 Have Courage and take Risks

It's not uncommon to fear change and the unknown. We're only human and it's human to suffer from a lack of nerve sometimes. As you work through this process I would like you to accept your own humanness.

Accept that it's alright to feel nervous, allow yourself to be comfortable with your 'discomfort', but then go beyond that and have the confidence to take perhaps the tiniest step towards the changes you want to make.

Making changes can result in successful or less successful outcomes. If you really want to transform your life you have to feel comfortable in accepting that sometimes things may not work out as you would like them to. However, don't forget, you'll learn from every action you take. As you go through the coaching process you'll stretch yourself, make a few mistakes along the way and learn from them. Once you accept that by living with uncertainty you will have the space to make the right choice, life becomes a lot easier. I want you to be willing to make mistakes and take steps into the unknown.

8 Notice Synchronicity

Is your life full of coincidences? Do you think about someone, only for the phone to ring and for you to find them on the other end of the line? Do you increasingly find yourself in the right place at the right time? Synchronicity, or meaningful coincidence, occurs in your life by means of perfectly timed events that just seem to happen out of the blue. These events may seem insignificant to you at the time, but when you look back later, they're often key turning-points.

Let Synchronicity Work for You

Synchronicity can be extremely helpful in moving your life forward. I want you to allow it to work for you. You can do this by paying close attention and becoming more aware of what's going on around you. As you become more present in the moment, you're more likely to look out for coincidences and start to notice synchronicities in your life. Pay attention to the people you keep bumping into. What do they say to you? Is there a topic that comes up time after time? Do you keep reading articles about the same subject? What keeps happening to you over and over again? Are there any key messages there for you?

Don't overlook the significance of coincidences. Ask yourself what they're showing you. They could propel you forwards more quickly than you might initially realize and are often a good indication that you're on the right path. As you open more to your intuition and inner wisdom, you'll notice synchronicities taking place more often and your life naturally gaining a steady momentum.

☆ What coincidences have occurred in your life over the last few weeks?

☆ What have you done to make the most of these events? Have you missed something significant?

☆ Make a list of the three people who seem to keep showing up most often in your life and what you intend to do to discover why.

9 ☆ Share your Successes and Celebrate

As you make progress, share your successes with your support team and acknowledge the roles they have played in helping you to move forward in your life. If you'd like to share any feedback, thoughts and results with me, I would love to hear from you. Your stories are a constant source of inspiration, ideas and energy!

☆ *Courage is very important. Like a muscle it is strengthened by use.* ☆

Ruth Gordon

Celebrate!

I mentioned the importance of celebration at the beginning and I'll mention it again now. Appreciate the wins in your life, both big and small, as this validates you and makes your transformation more meaningful and fulfilling.

Live your life to the full, live it well, have fun and capture the joy in each moment.

Congratulations on completing this phase of your life transformation. I would like to wish you all the best for a fulfilling life!

Carole Gaskell

PS If you'd like to stay connected with thoughts and ideas on transforming your life, you can subscribe to my free e-mail newsletter by visiting my website: www.lifecoaching-company.co.uk or e-mailing me at info@lifecoaching-company.co.uk.

☆ *In each of us are places where we have never gone. Only by pressing the limits do you ever find them.* ☆

Joyce Brothers

Make
www.thorsonselement.com
your online sanctuary

Get online information, inspiration and guidance to help you on the path to physical and spiritual well-being. Drawing on the integrity and vision of our authors and titles, and with health advice, articles, astrology, tarot, a meditation zone, author interviews and events listings, www.thorsonselement.com is a great alternative to help create space and peace in our lives.

So if you've always wondered about practising yoga, following an allergy-free diet, using the tarot or getting a life coach, we can point you in the right direction.

www.thorsonselement.com • www.thorsonselement.com • www.thorsonselement.com